UBC RECEIPT

Deposit on Graduation Photographs received from:

NAME: _Maureen Cere..._

SCHOOL: _____

DATE: _____ MAY 1 1 2002

AMOUNT RECEIVED: _____ 65

☐ MASTERCARD

☐ DIRECT PAYMENT

Your photographs will be delivered to your High School after the entire grad class has been photographed. University and individual sittings will be delivered by mail. Please take your previews home for one to two weeks only. Yearbook and composite deadlines have already been set for your school. Your deposit will be credited entirely to your order when you return your previews to us for re-ordering. Previews not returned within two weeks, will be considered purchased. All forfeited deposits will be applied to previews and folders in your possession, not to reorders. Sales taxes are additional. Any balance due will be billed to you directly.

UBC PORTRAIT PACKAGES

THE UBC STUDIO MASTER (MAX. 6 POSES) SAVE $217.45 $299.95
Plus up to 16 previews from your sitting and one 8-up Presentation Folder.

1 — 16 x 20   1 — 10 x 13   3 — 8 x 10   4 — 5 x 7   8 — 4 x 5   24 JUMBO WALLETS

THE UBC GRADUATION SPECIAL (MAX. 5 POSES) SAVE $187.50 $239.95
Plus up to 16 previews from your sitting and one 8-up Presentation Folder.

1 — 10 x 13   2 — 8 x 10   6 — 5 x 7   8 — 4 x 5   24 JUMBO WALLETS (2x3)

THE UBC CONTEMPORARY (MAX. 4 POSES) SAVE $156.34 $199.95
Plus 12 previews from your sitting and one 8-up Presentation Folder.

1 — 10 x 13   2 — 8 x 10   4 — 5 x 7   6 — 4 x 5   20 JUMBO WALLETS (2x3)

THE UBC GRAD (MAX. 3 POSES) SAVE $54.64 $169.95
Plus 8 previews from your sitting and one 8-up Presentation Folder.

1 — 10 x 13   2 — 8 x 10   2 — 5 x 7   4 — 4 x 5   12 JUMBO WALLETS (2x3)

THE UBC GRADUATE SAVE $35.80 $129.95
(ONLY 1 POSE)

2 — 8 x 10   4 — 5 x 7   4 — 4 x 5

THE UBC SCHOLAR $69.95
(ONLY 1 POSE) SAVE $19.90

1 — 8 x 10   2 — 5 x 7   4 — 4 x 5

AGREEMENT FOR PHOTOGRAPHIC SERVICES

The following agreement must be signed before The Artona Group Inc. will perform any photographic services. The undersigned understands and agrees that:

1) In accordance with Canadian Federal Copyright Law, section C-42 of the Copyright Act and as endorsed by the Professional Photographers of Canada and the Professional Photographers of British Columbia, the copyright of all photographic works created by The Artona Group Inc. rests with The Artona Group Inc.

2) As the legal holder of the copyright of such photographs, all rights are reserved by The Artona Group Inc. unless released in writing. Any infringements of these rights, including copying or duplicating in any form will result in persecution as provided by Canadian Law.

UBC Photography

PREVIEWS

All previews and folders are the property of the Artona Group Inc. unless you wish to purchase them. When you return your previews and folder to the studio within fourteen days (two weeks), your deposit will be credited entirely to your order. Previews and folders not returned within that time will be considered purchased. Previews chosen for ordering must be returned to the studio with your order. These are required for retouchers to have a reference point to work from.

• All reorders are subject to a $6.42 handling charge
• You will receive a group of photographs to look at commonly known as previews or proofs.
• Each preview has a digital number on the front. This is called a *pose number*.
• Previews are not retouched. Judge them only for expression, as the colour and tone will be corrected on your final portraits.
• Your previews are not retouched, nor may they necessarily be the exact colour balance.

8 Previews - $46.00 12 Previews (with 8-up folder) - $57.00 16 Previews (with 8-up folder) - $68.00

A LA CARTE

• Various portrait sheets may be ordered in addition to or instead of portrait packages.
• Only one pose per portrait sheet may be ordered. However, if 2 or more of the same portrait sheets are ordered, each may be of a different pose.

1 — 16" x 20" $89.95	2 — 5" x 7" (Both of 1 pose) $29.95
(Mounted Wall Portrait)	4 — 4" x 5" (All 4 of 1 pose) $29.95
1 — 10" x 13" $59.95	8 — Jumbo Wallets (All 8 of 1 pose)
(Mounted Wall Portrait)	.... $29.95
1 — 8" x 10" $29.95	Wallet Special (All 40 of 1 pose) $54.95

RETOUCHING

• Once you have chosen your poses, every negative goes through a retouching process. A new photograph is printed from your retouched negative. Each photograph is then further retouched completing this unique method of softening or eliminating blemishes.
• Retouching does not straighten teeth, remove braces, take out wrinkles or circles under eyes, correct clothing, remove eyeglass glare nor eliminate frizzy or loose hair.
Retouching is not a magical solution to all imperfections.
• Airbrushing is not available at the prices quoted here; nor is it necessary.

FOLDERS

• Protect your valuable photographs with Artona's exclusive presentation folders. These folders are not available in any store.

1 — 8" x 10" $4.95	1 — 4" x 5" $2.95
1 — 5" x 7" $3.95	8-up Presentation Folder $7.95

THE ARTONA GROUP INC.
MASTERS OF PHOTOGRAPHIC AND ELECTRONIC IMAGING
353 West 7th Avenue, Vancouver, B.C. V5Y 1M2
Telephone: (604) 872-7272 Fax: (604) 872-7273

Proper English

THE LANGUAGE LIBRARY

Series editor: David Crystal

Also published in the series:

Ronald Carter and Walter Nash	*Seeing Through Language*
Florin Coulmas	*The Writing Systems of the World*
David Crystal	*A Dictionary of Linguistics and Phonetics (Forth Edition)*
J. A. Cuddon	*A Dictionary of Literary Terms and Literary Theory (Fourth Edition)*
Ronald Wardhaugh	*How Conversation Works*
Ronald Wardhaugh	*Investigating Language*

Proper English

Myths and Misunderstandings about Language

Ronald Wardhaugh

First published 1999

2 4 6 8 10 9 7 5 3 1

Blackwell Publishers Inc.
350 Main Street
Malden, Massachusetts 02148
USA

Blackwell Publishers Ltd
108 Cowley Road
Oxford OX4 1JF
UK

Library of Congress Cataloging-in-Publication Data

Wardhaugh, Ronald.
  Proper English : myths and misunderstandings about language / Ronald Wardhaugh.
    p. cm. — (The language library)
  Includes bibliographical references and index.
  ISBN 0–631–21268–X (hb : alk. paper). — ISBN 0–631–21269–8 (pbk : alk. paper)
  1. English language—Standardization. 2. English language—Variation. 3. English language—Usage. I. Title. II. Series.
PE1074.7.W37   1999
428—dc21   98–24577
                                                                             CIP

British Library Cataloguing in Publication Data

A CIP catalogue record for this book is available from the British Library.

Typeset in 10½ on 13 pt Meridien
by Ace Filmsetting Ltd, Frome, Somerset
Printed in Great Britain by T.J. International, Padstow, Cornwall

This book is printed on acid-free paper.

For Laura Wardhaugh,
my mother,
on her ninetieth birthday

And for Margaret, Victoria, and Christopher,
her great-grandchildren.

Contents

Preface

Language plays an important role in the lives of all of us and is our most distinctive human possession. We might expect, therefore, to be well-informed about it. The truth is we are not. Many statements we believe to be true about language are likely as not false. Many of the questions we concern ourselves with are either unanswerable and therefore not really worth asking or betray a serious misunderstanding of the nature of language. Most of us have learned many things about language from others, but generally the wrong things. More likely than not we have acquired ideas and beliefs that do not have facts to back them. However, we often insist on handing these on to others in the firm conviction that we are thereby handing on wisdom and perhaps even safeguarding the very language itself.

Linguists have been studying language for many years and know that many popular beliefs about language are false and that much we are taught about language is misdirected. They also know how difficult it is to effect change. This book is an attempt to show why so many of us hold the beliefs we do hold and why we should question these and seek to replace them.

I have chosen to write in what I hope is an accessible style. My purpose is quite explicit. I want to bring to the "common reader" an awareness of why it is we believe what we believe about language, do what we do with it, and insist on passing on these beliefs and practices to the next generation. If we are to change how we view language, we must first understand what it is we must change: a set of beliefs and practices in which language issues are either completely misunderstood or thoroughly confused with other issues.

I am particularly concerned with the kinds of observations we have become accustomed to about English. Our language is the most important language in the world. I say that unashamedly and with no feeling of linguistic chauvinism, for I believe that at the end of the second millennium it is a fact. However, there is so much nonsense written about English (and, unfortunately in it) that I intend this book as a mild "corrective." I admire "good English." I am not sure about everything that is given the label "proper English." I invite the reader to find out why that is so in the pages that follow.

You taught me language; and my profit on't
Is, I know how to curse; the red plague rid you
For learning me your language!
   Caliban to Prospero
   William Shakespeare's *The Tempest*

Wayward Words

Near the beginning of William Shakespeare's *The Tempest* we find the magician Prospero in conversation with the monster Caliban. Prospero has just told Caliban how good he has been to him, particularly in giving him language: "I endowed thy purposes with words that made them known." However, Caliban has a much different view of what has happened to him. Language has been a curse that has removed him from his natural exist-ence, and he proceeds to berate Prospero for "learning me your language."

Like Caliban, we have all learned a language, but we have not been taught it in the usual sense of the word *teach*. In that pro-cess we have learned – and in this case that word *taught* is en-tirely appropriate – a lot about language. Much that we have learned is not particularly useful, some may be harmful, and only a little is likely to be helpful. What we might try to do is sort out which bits of learning are which, and at the same time ac-count for why it is that we persist in handing down from gen-eration to generation such a rag-bag collection of fact and fantasy about language. Why do we experience our language the way we do? How do we account for the fact that while we are learn-ing to use that language, we also learn many things about it that cause us so much anxiety? But why, too, can we not safely ignore what we do learn?

1 Making Less Stupid Mistakes

We do not have to look far to find evidence that supports Caliban's feelings about language, that it is something to complain about publicly. We need to go no further than our daily newspapers, the books we read, and to those – and they are many – who feel free to comment on language to find ample evidence that there is something wrong about the way we often use words.

Thinking about such matters, I decided to note some of my own reactions to language. As a linguist interested in the social uses of language, I try to attend closely to what I hear and read. However, I concerned myself on this occasion with my non-linguistic reactions, those judgmental responses I make to the use of language around me. Let me illustrate. One of the items that caught my attention was a series of letters in a Toronto newspaper the *Globe and Mail*. A columnist's sentence *Victory can go to he who yells loudest* brought a letter from a correspondent who insisted that the *he* should be *him*. This letter brought still another letter, which said that the original *he* was correct, and then a final letter appeared arguing for *him* once more. Every grammar of standard English tells us that the original sentence should have read *Victory can go to him who yells loudest* because, as the final letter writer stated, the pronoun *him* is the grammatical object of the preposition *to*, and *who yells loudest* is a relative clause modifying that pronoun. What is surprising about the whole incident, apart from the linguistic insecurity – at least in standard English – of the original writer and of the second letter writer, is that a newspaper such as the *Globe and Mail*, with the claims it makes about its being Canada's "newspaper of record," printed the original "error," that letter-writing to newspapers on points of usage is such a popular sport, and that those who write such letters are often poorly informed but nevertheless quite sure they are correct in their views.

Another series of letters in the *Globe and Mail* was concerned with a statement from a prominent investment advisor that *We open all our meetings with a prayer because it helps us to make less stupid mistakes*. In one view the effect of such praying fell short of ensuring that the advisor himself always communicated in the kind of English that the prayed-to deity is believed to approve. Or perhaps the particular activity he was engaged in was temporarily out of divine favor! Predictably, the letters dealt with the use of *less* as a modifier of a countable noun like *mistakes*. One correspondent suggested that the investment advisor pray harder next time so as not to make such an "error," but others declared their support for the use. The most amusing comment was that perhaps the investment advisor had meant exactly what he had said if he were to be credited with using the language "properly": if you prayed, the mistakes you made might still be stupid but they would perhaps be less stupid than those you might make if you did not pray at all! It was an entertaining discussion but there was a point to it. I am very particular about my own uses of *less* and *fewer*. I do make fewer mistakes with *less*; indeed I try to make none at all and have willingly straitjacketed myself here in my use of *less* and *fewer*.

Another series of letters concerned a poster on display at that time in Toronto which said *It's you who counts the most*. The correspondence included two letters that launched into a discussion of some of the grammatical characteristics of the sentence. One correspondent went so far as to insist that *counts* is a plural verb because it ends in an *s*, thus providing proof that letters to the editor are suitable places for signed, public displays of ignorance. How can you be so wrong yet believe you are so right?

Concurrently, my mail brought me a book produced by a firm of financial consultants which, among other things, informed me that if "you willingly or knowingly flaunt the law," the penalties can be severe. However, real-life experience tells me that those who indeed flaunt the law do quite well out of it and, it is tempting to add, too few who flout the law get caught. The problem here is with *flaunt* and *flout*. These words are commonly "confused" so that *flaunt* is often, as here, used in the sense of *flout*. Many people consider that standard English requires the strict separation of the meanings of these words. The difference is a kind of shibboleth today for many purists, i.e., those who think that "language standards" are declining and must be upheld. We may remember that a shibboleth is a fatal mistake, for Judges 12:

5–16 in the Old Testament tells us how the Gileadites slaughtered certain Ephraimites because they pronounced *shibboleth* as *sibboleth*. *Webster's Third New International Dictionary* of 1961 (which from now on I will refer to as *Webster's Third*) acknowledges that the battle to keep the two words apart is largely lost because one of the meanings given there for *flaunt* is "to treat contemptuously." The question at issue here is who is right. Are the purists right? Is the dictionary right? And how should a reader react to *flaunt* used in this way?

I myself learned the *flaunt–flout* distinction from a copy editor. In the manuscript of one of my books I used *flaunt* for the purists' *flout*. This sharp-eyed copy editor "corrected" me. As we will see, sharp-eyed copy editors are very important people. Can you imagine what published works would be like without them? I suspect they would be somewhat different: standard non-copy-edited English, which is what most writers write. If they do so, why are the changes made that are made? What function does copy editing serve and who wins and who loses from the attention copy editors give to our words? One obvious group of winners are copy editors. Another group are their teachers, but where exactly does the teaching of copy-editing skills fit within education in our language?

Reading a detective novel written by one of England's best-known mystery writers, Ruth Rendell, I find Detective Chief Inspector Wexford replying to his niece's question *What have you been up to Uncle Reg?* with *Me?* and my author adding *said Wexford ungrammatically*. How else could he have replied and stayed in character, this unpretentious country policeman? How could he possibly have replied *I*, considering the way the question was asked, the domestic setting in which it was asked, the characters having just finished lunch at home, the kinds of people they are, and, above all, the way people actually do use the language, quite possibly the distinguished mystery writer herself? What is the point of adding *ungrammatically*? What kind of language game are we witnessing here? Lest it seem that only female mystery writers are prone to such linguistic concerns, we cannot ignore Colin Dexter's Inspector Morse of Oxford. An unsuccessful student of Classics in his time at the university, Morse, as his assistant Sergeant Lewis knows only too well, is an expert on three things other than detection: classical music, beer, and the English language. Is there a sub-text in these books on law and order, that words must also behave properly?

It is not only newspapers and books that contain uses of language that attract my attention. A television advertisement makes me aware of *Canadian Sports Fishing at It's Best*, a television magazine declares that *TV recycles it's past*, and a newspaper headline proclaims that *It's time Canadian film industry rediscovered it's audience*. What should I make of this? What does it tell me? Is it a sign that our language is in a state of rapid decline with disorder everywhere? Or is it a sign that "editorial standards" are declining? Or am I witnessing an artificial and inconsistent distinction that happens to be in the written language in the process of disappearing? Such questions occur to me because I have heard them raised thoughout my life. They are part of my experience with language. I would not have asked them had I not been indoctrinated into caring about language in a certain way. I also know that others share my cares.

The *Globe and Mail* introduced a new stylebook near the end of 1990 with considerable fanfare. Within days of the publication of that stylebook, one headline in the paper declared *Habs Should Have Drank a Toast to Discipline*, another read *The person they are most likely to kill is themself*, and a feature article informed us that *Kadokawa could care less about such carping*. If those in control of the newspaper felt that there were issues of style that they should deal with, apparently they were not these issues.

Returning to the example of *could care less*, should I believe Wlliam Safire in *On Language* when he says of this expression that it "seems to be petering out."? The widespread use of this phrase suggests that Safire may well be mistaken in his facts. But, more interesting – or should that be *interestingly*? – how should we go about ascertaining the facts in such a case? How can we distinguish facts from opinions in matters to do with language? And, if we can, which is to be master? Is the answer uniquivocal?

In a magazine included with another Toronto paper, the *Toronto Star*, a columnist repeated, approvingly, someone who had declared that *"basically* . . . isn't in the dictionary." But surely a dictionary that omits *basically* is not doing its job! John Simon, a noted critic of current linguistic usage who thinks that it is up to people like him to bring order and discipline to the language, tells us in *Paradigms Lost* that English "clearly prefers *You are better than I* to *You are better than me.*" *Clearly prefers* is a strong statement but where is the evidence for it? What is the authority for it other than Simon's assertion? How do we read the mind and fathom the preferences of "English"? What justifies a workshop announcement on the topic "Grammar and Usage for the Business Professional" that it will help those who attend avoid the "3 mistakes to never make" (*sic*) and "the most common pronunciation errors," and "identify 100 words that even the best communicators misuse and misspell"? There is obviously a considerable – and very profitable – market for this type of enterprise, but why does it exist at all? However, even as I ask this question, I must acknowledge that I have not been unaffected. I do not speak and write today as I did at mid-century. My language has been shaped by learning about language but less by learning about it as a linguist than by learning about it as a talking, writing, social being.

Here are a few more examples of usages that caught my attention during my period of deliberate observation and self-observation. An article in the *New Yorker* contained the following sentences: "I remembered a rather long lunch with the sociologist Hector Castillo when he had said that the obsessive question for him was whom to blame for all the garbage pickers' misery. In the bright light of Mrs. Lopez's home, an even more disturbing question arose: whom to thank for her new surroundings?" Those two instances of *whom* jarred me. If such stylistic infelicity is the price we must pay for using *whom* "correctly," it is much too high. I follow William Safire's advice on the use of *who* and *whom* in *Coming to Terms*: "When *whom* is correct, recast the sentence" (but not necessarily as he advises). I did, however, like that magazine's preference for *none* followed by a plural verb in *none are going* and *none now sell* in another issue, but I am sure this use jarred some readers.

In Marge Piercy's novel *Summer People* I find: "He had been one of those Juilliard students whom everyone said would make it in the cut-throat concert circuit." How did that *whom* get there?

A. N. Wilson's *Gentleman in England* contains the following exchange: "'And two very handsome children – Lionel, whom I gather is doing very well at Harcourt.' 'Who do you gather that from?'" Is this slipshod writing and slipshod editing, or is it an accurate observation of the insecurity of one speaker with *whom* and the freedom of the other with *who*? And what should I think of a person reported in a business magazine to have said "at least half of them are gonna buy the book to find out whom they're dealing with," with *whom* flanked by *gonna* and *they're*? Is this good reporting, bad speaking, or bad editing? If it is the first, what are we to make of the speaker, and if one of the latter two, where does our concept of "bad" come from?

In contrast to the above, the *me* in a "Talk of the Town" piece in the *New Yorker* seems just right: "Is it me, or has New York City been producing more than its usual crop of apocalyptic images?" When Barry Broadfoot in *Six War Years, 1939–45* recounts what a soldier under fire said: "He was shooting at me as if I was a German. It's him or me," that seems to be completely appropriate language for the circumstances. How could "He was shooting at me as if I were a German. It's he or I" possibly be any better?

Speaking of a basketball coach who had rejoined a team, another *New Yorker* writer informs us that: "Walter Kennedy embraced the prodigal" and, while this is the way *prodigal* is frequently used, it is a word like *decimate*, another favorite subject of writers of letters to newpapers, that many people have strong feelings about. When a dental hygienist says to me *Open widely*, should I just open my mouth without comment but not perhaps without wondering whether this is something they teach in dental-hygiene school? Or was an English teacher responsible? Or should I try to point out that *Open wide*, like *Drive slow*, has strong historical justification?

Finally, reading the 1996 Reith Lectures given by Jean Aitchison, the Rupert Murdoch Professor of Language and Communication at Oxford, published as *The Language Web*, I find this sentence: "Moving on to the the nineteenth century, proper behaviour was a major concern to a lot of people." In the twentieth century so are dangling modifiers to many of their descendants. The sentence is perfectly comprehensible even with its dangling modifier but I must confess that I would not write a similar sentence, having learned to avoid this "error."

Those were and are some of my reactions to a variety of language matters. A mixed bag but there they are. Others will have different reactions, for no-one reading these last few pages will have failed to react to their contents. The important isssue is why this is so. How did we learn to have such reactions?

We are assailed with advertisements for elocution lessons, speech correction, accent modification, and grammar correction, all addressed to native speakers and all designed to create an impression that our language is in trouble. This kind of material is not just a contemporary phenomenon either. In 1856 Walton Burgess published a book called *Five Hundred Mistakes of Daily Occurrence in Speaking, Pronouncing, and Writing the English Language, Corrected.* In 1875 came L. P. Meredith's *Every-day Errors of Speech,* in 1886 Harlan Ballard's *Handbook of Blunders*, and in 1889 William Hodgson's *Errors in the Use of English*, which in its Introduction claims to be a "book founded on actual blunders, verified by chapter-and-verse reference, and gathered in a course of desultory reading over the last thirty years." The last author's only regret was that his work was not "exhaustive."

These books discuss "problems" like using *learn* with the meaning of *teach*, *decimate* with the meaning *destroy*, *aggravate* with the meaning *annoy*, and *nice* with the meaning *agreeable*. They also discuss *between you and I, creek* pronounced to rhyme with *brick* and *burst* to rhyme with *bust*, the "failure" to pronounce the first *r* in *February*, *chimney* pronounced as *chimley*, the use of the word *pants* for *trousers*, and numerous other issues dear to the hearts of those who profess to be the caretakers of our language.

We are all subject to this kind of instruction in the language, sometimes formally more often informally. I have mentioned my own experience with *flaunt* and *flout*. I remember too as a young grammar-school boy in northeast England telling my English teacher that I was starving when I was very cold one day. He told me that *starving* meant "hungry" whereas to me it also meant "to be really cold." I desisted from using the word in that last sense only to find out years later that my meaning – something like "dying from exposure" – had a long historical justification. My meaning was still very much alive in the variety of English that I had learned as a child but it did not exist in the standard variety favored in my school.

Another early recollection comes from the time I was five or six years old. A slightly older boy – therefore one much more sophisticated in the ways of the world than me (or should that be *I*?) – told me that in Canada there was a mouse that was even taller than a man. We both pronounced *mouse* to rhyme with *loose* (as we also did *house*). I was amazed to hear that a mouse could be so big. When I eventually did see a moose, I knew he was right in one sense but by then my *mouse* and *house* no longer rhymed with *loose*. My accent had changed dramatically. However, I do still occasionally pronounce *book* with the vowel of *moon* and differentiating between *walk* and *work* can be a problem because I have to remember to make them rhyme with *fork* and *shirk* respectively. There is a conscious part still to some of my language behavior.

My vocabulary and grammar are less problematic than my pronunciaton. (My spelling is almost entirely North American.) So far as vocabulary is concerned I long ago gave up using *colored*, *negro*, and *black* in favor of *Afro-American*, but I am now in the process of replacing the latter with *African-American*. I try to write 'non-sexist" prose but must have failed at that task when a strongly feminist student from an American university sent me a critique of one of my books, which she claimed was thoroughly "sexist" in its language and orientation. I must confess that I could not see her point. We were obviously using words very differently. Although I had tried to be "politically correct," I had apparently failed. However, can any language, except that of pure mathematics, be thoroughly neutral? I must confess too that a lot of prose I read is just as impervious to interpretaton as that critique. As I wander through bookstores looking at what is for sale, I can make little sense of much of what I see and no sense at all of some. In particular, the so-called New Age and occult sections are a complete mystery to me. I can parse the sentences but there is no other meaningful connection. So many words, words, words! And yet such books sell.

We are surrounded by language. We use it, we hear it, and we comment on it. We cannot escape language and probably would not want to. But words exact a price. We should know what that price is. What we have learned about language is part of our knowledge of language. It is not an unimportant part to be dismissed as unworthy of serious study and informed comment.

2 Degeneracy and Disorder

Every year we find published either a new book on English usage telling us how to correct our errant ways or an older one brought up to date with the same purpose. We find the same discussions of the poor use of language in programs on radio and television, the same letters to editors, and the same complaints about the poverty of the language used by the young. Yet, where is the hard evidence that the English language is any "worse" at the end of the twentieth century than it was in the 1960s, the 1930s, or at the century's beginning?

Here are two such opinions on the current state of our language and those who use it drawn at random from many possibilities. The first is from *Correcting Your English* by Harry Blamires. He says that "this is a good time to explore error in English usage. There is a lot of it about" and: "We shall begin to write well by learning to recognise bad English and to avoid the practices which make it bad." The second is from what many would consider to be a more exalted source, the Prince of Wales, who in 1989 wondered: "what is it about our country and our society that our language has become so impoverished, so sloppy and so limited . . .?" Badness, impoverishment, sloppiness, and limitations: these are typical comments of doomsayers. But who is to cast the first stone? Are we not all guilty to some extent? Or are there some creatures of perfection?

I found a possible answer to that last question while reading *The Quark and the Jaguar* by the Nobel laureate in physics Murray Gell-Mann. Writing of his early years and talking of his father born in Austria-Hungary, Gell-Mann tells how his father learned English as a young adult in the United States. His "grammar and pronunciation became perfect." Gell-Mann adds: "When I knew him, the only way one might have guessed he was foreign-born was by noticing that he never made any mistakes." What an interesting idea: natives make mistakes; non-natives sometimes do not! Gell-Mann seems to find nothing strange in what he says. However, I find the whole idea mind-boggling: something native is characterized by "mistakes" and something non-native by their absence. And this from a Nobel laureate in science.

When we look closely at statements made about ordinary language use, we see that they are almost always filled with forecasts of doom and gloom. The goddess Progress does not hold court here. Commentators on the state of the language find nothing to praise in what they see and much that should cause us to despair. If each language has a golden age, unfortunately that age for English lies far in the past, either in Shakespeare's time or somewhat later during the reign of Queen Anne in the early eighteenth century. If we are to believe what we are told, the language has been degenerating ever since. Such opinions have been voiced constantly, Jonathan Swift and Samuel Johnson – at least until the latter did some serious work on the language for his famous dictionary – being two of its most famous exponents. Every reasonably sized bookstore will have books written by the latest language down-sayers, and most newspapers print from time to time the letters of a "Disgusted" or an "Outraged," someone who has become incensed at one or other usage. But has the world degenerated linguistically? Is there any evidence to suggest that all the complaints made about the "linguistic decline and fall" of the language and all the caring about "standards" that has been expressed have had the slightest effect on the language itself? And why do we allow ourselves to be drawn into such discussions?

If we prize facts rather than opinions, we must ask whether we can accept conclusions such as Richard Grant White's in 1870 in his very influential book *Words and Their Uses*: "There is a misuse of words which can be justified by no authority, however great, by no usage, however general." These are strong words. Over a century later a modern critic, best left nameless, made an even stronger assertion: "Abuse of language . . . leads . . . to a deterioration of moral values and standards of living." A recent exemplar of this genre is *Words Fail Us* by Bob Blackburn, a Canadian writer and columnist during much of the 1980s for *Books in Canada.* His concern is with the "errors and undesirable practices that have offended my eye and ear in recent years." Very bravely, he goes so far as to apologize for an error in print for which he was himself responsible: "The offending writer was I," he says, a sentence which though grammatically correct from the purist's point of view is one, if we have any ear at all for the language, we probably would not want to use or have our students use.

Blackburn passes out praise and condemnation, and is much more comfortable with the latter than with the former: "For some centuries, concerned people have tried mightily to codify rules designed to help English-speaking people understand one another. For the last half-century, unconcerned people have been wantonly frustrating this work." *Wantonly* is a strong word: *excessive, unchaste, lewd, lustful, heedless,* and *unchecked* are some synonyms of *wanton* so to be "unconcerned" about language matters that excite Blackburn is to exhibit one or more such characteristics. These are harsh, judgmental words. Blackburn fails to tell us how English-speaking people managed to communicate with each other before "concerned' people undertook their efforts. Did King Alfred have to eke out what he said with gestures and, if he did so, how do we account for his military and political successes and the *Anglo-Saxon Chronicle*?

Perhaps the editors of the *New Yorker* should have heeded what Blackburn writes, quite ungrammatically we should observe, about *none*: "*none* means no one, and the fact that its misuse can be traced back more than 1,000 years, that its misuse is widespread, and that its misuse is condoned by many authorities, have nothing to do with the basic fact that IT IS A SINGULAR PRONOUN." (A consistent purist would write *has* not *have* because the antecedent is *fact,* a singular noun.) Even the *Oxford English Dictionary* (or *OED*) must suffer Blackburn's scorn along with the language it has chronicled because "as everyone . . . knows . . . (it) is for the most part a chronicle of the abuses the English language has suffered at the hands of the likes of Shakespeare and Milton, who had the ill fortune to be writing before the rules of usage had been codified properly." Poor Shakespeare, poor James Murray, poor you and me, but hurrah for Blackburn, telling it like it is, pulling no punches, and tilting so proudly at windmills on our behalf!

Bold assertions of the kind favored by Blackburn and others of his persuasion too often replace evidence on matters that could possibly count in our lives. Why do publishers publish such tracts and people buy them? The answer is simple: there is a strong market for them and people are interested in the topics they address. As David Crystal found out in his 1986 BBC series on language, people have strong opinions about language use. He found the most frequent complaints to be about *between you and I*, the split infinitive, misplaced *only* (*I only have one*), *none are*, *different than*, sentence-ending prepositions, improper uses of *shall* and *will* for the future, the sentence adverb *hopefully*, failure to use *whom*, and the double negative. For many people such matters as these lie at the very heart of English grammar. They have lain there for centuries and they do not go away. It is this last fact that makes them so interesting to us. If they do not go away, they must be important to us for reasons that extend far beyond language alone.

3 Is it *Color* or *Colour*?

It is possible to focus on discrete parts of the language and look at the level of public interest there. Let us take English spelling as a simple example. Why has correct spelling assumed the importance it has in our society? Poor spelling was ridiculed as long ago as the sixteenth century. In his Preface to *The English Schoole-Maister* of 1596 Edmund Coote mentioned how some people are so "ashamed" of their spelling that they will not write to their friends. Two centuries later Lord Chesterfield in *Letters to His Son* warned the young man against misspelling words because of the social consequences. Why do we place so high a value on the ability to spell? Should an inability to spell certain words mark a person as being uneducated? Or is the ability to spell a trivial accomplishment after all?

A former colleague of mine freely admits to being a terrible speller. He has written several successful books but realizes that spelling has nothing to do with writing ability and that correct spelling can safely be left to his publishers. This view distinguishes the important, scholarly, creative task from one that takes no great skill at all, that is, seeing that the words used are eventually spelled correctly, a task many otherwise uneducated teenagers are able to do quite well. President Kennedy was also an abysmal speller but we would not know that from reading his published works. (Of course, like many others in similar circumstances, Kennedy did not write much of what he is credited with, but that is another issue: what we can get credit for if we have power and influence.)

The attitude of my former colleague toward spelling is unusual. More usual is the concern that a group of examiners at Oxford University in 1983 voiced about the spellings that extremely bright undergraduates used in examinations, spellings like *acomodate, advisor, concensus, developement, fulfill, irrelevence, occured, practiced, the practises, privelege, proffessional, seige, sieze, seperate, supercede,* and *willfull.* (Note my own use of *advisor* just a few pages ago.) Most of us have our own lists of words that we are on the look out for either in print or, if we are teachers, in our students' writing. A few of mine are *accommodate,* the *principal–principle, its–it's,* and *compliment–complement* distinctions, *vocal cords, pronunciation, diphthong, grammar,* and *guttural.* However, if one of these words is misspelled, is the meaning misunderstood? The importance of spelling goes far beyond anything that might be said to be purely linguistic or communicative; it is a social and cultural matter.

We can see that this is so when we consider how spellings like those that follow arouse controversy: *lite beer, dialog, thru, nite,* and *kwik.* Are advertisers subverting an already endangered language when they spell words in such ways? What would we lose if we accepted spellings like *kaos, hav, kat, anser, rench, rek,* and *giv* from children and also allowed such spellings to find their way into print? We might add *accomodate* (or *acomodate)* and a few others from the Oxford examiners' list. Should the possibility that we can have more than one spelling for a word be any more alarming than the possibility that we can have more than one pronunciation? Or is an unvarying spelling system somehow different, a bit of language order that we require to buttress social order? Would some choice in spelling wreak further havoc on the language? Where do we examine such issues and the assumptions behind them?

Anyone who has dealt with a variety of publishers will know how arbitrary many of the "rules" are. There are preferred "house" spellings and rules for lots of other things too: names, titles, hyphenation, punctuation, word usages, etc. I remember that in the editing process of the first book I wrote I often used *which* to introduce restrictive relative clauses, as in *The task which confronts a reader is not an easy one.* My American copy editor changed all such uses of *which* to *that* in conformity with the prescribed house use so eliminating my British preference. However, sensible editors do not treat such prescriptions as absolutes, being well aware that the language has a life of its own, one that sometimes cannot be so readily contained.

Canadians have a particular problem in such matters, positioned as they are between two spelling systems, the American and the British. Which do we choose? The differences are quite minimal but the passions aroused can be considerable. Should a "real Anglo-Canadian" write *color* or *colour, theater* or *theatre, judgment* or *judgement*? (Of course, there is the occurrence of *jewelery* rather than either the British *jewellery* or the American *jewelry*. This *jewelery* is a not uncommon spelling, being found, for example, on an elaborate sign on a store on one of Toronto's main streets. But perhaps this is not a Canadian compromise at all, just the consequence of not knowing either of the other two spellings!)

Even the most anglophile Canadian rejects *tyre, gaol, kerb, recognise, waggon, connexion,* and *aluminium* but may take up arms against perceived Americanisms to the extent that we find occasional overcorrections like *perimetre* and *Ann Arbour* or a letter to the editor decrying the spelling *Labor Day.* This last writer believed that the *-our* ending "makes more sense phonetically" than the *-or* ending. One motivation of the *Globe and Mail*'s 1990 stylebook seems to have been political: to make the spelling in that newspaper less American than before at a time when, because of certain political and economic changes in Canada, which incidentally the newspaper strongly favored, Canada appeared to be becoming more dependent on the United States than before. The style changes were designed, in the newspaper's words, "to keep pace with changes in the language that reflect new attitudes and sensitivities in Canadian society." Extralinguistic factors were clearly at work.

The above comment about the pronunciation of *labor* raises the issue of whether or not the spelling of a word should guide us in its pronunciation. There is a strong belief that it should, not, as was the case in ancient India, so that the exact pronunciation of religious texts could be preserved over the years, but rather because many people feel that we derive our pronunciations of words from their spellings. In this view it is the written variety of the language that is the basic form not the spoken variety. Language is what is written not what is spoken. Consequently, we find people saying that *debt* has a silent *b*, we are exhorted not to "drop" the final *g* in a word like *going*, and children are taught that some letters "say their own names." To anyone with a good understanding of the nature of language, such statements are bizarre. However, they are an important part of our language lore.

We are informed that English is not a "phonetic" language. Perhaps the English spelling system does not represent English as it is spoken as closely as the German spelling system represents spoken German, but it does get quite close, unlike Chinese, for example, which makes almost no attempt at all to do so. Yet all languages, English, German, and Chinese, are phonetic – all are spoken – so when English is described as not being "phonetic," this word is being given a meaning that is not at all helpful if we want to try to understand how English is pronounced, how it is spelled, and the relationship between the sounds of English and the spelling system of English. Once again it is important that we find out some facts about the relationship of sounds with spellings rather than keep on repeating obvious falsehoods and misrepresenting the issues.

4 Regarding *Irregardless*

Why do dictionaries play an important role in our lives when language matters come to the fore? Why are they treated as the ultimate sources of authority in such matters just as various religious books are treated in other matters. People use dictionaries to settle arguments. But where does the authority of the dictionary come from? There are also various dictionaries and they do not give us the same information and answers about the language and the issues we seek to resolve. So which dictionary should we rely on and why? Dictionaries provide a kind of order and authority for our language – even if in some cases that order is little more than an alphabetical listing and the authority may be questioned – but are they really to be trusted?

Dictionaries give us information about words. The existence of dictionaries reinforces a strong belief many people have that a language is merely a collection of words. We learn a language by learning its words: how to pronounce them; how to put them together; what exactly they mean; how to spell them; and so on. Furthermore, if a word is not in the dictionary we must assume that it is not in the language. This is the argument widely used with *irregardless*: it is not in certain dictionaries so it is not in the language no matter how often we actually come across it in speech, possibly even use it ourselves. Moreover, if some dictionary-maker puts it in a dictionary, that inclusion is a mistake because *irregardless* is not a legitimate word because it is not in other dictionaries, a completely circular argument. The real issue here is that of deciding on the legitimacy of words. Who should decide which words are to go into dictionaries and what criteria should they use? Should a dictionary include that word from *Mary Poppins*, *supercalifragilisticexpialidocious*? If yes, why, and, if no, why not?

Dictionaries usually try to give us an objective record of the language but there is sometimes disagreement about the concept of "objectivity" in matters to do with language. Dictionary-makers know the kinds of judgments they are called on to make. They know how many react to their efforts. Not all dictionaries are alike in the way they deal with words, particularly with words that have proved to be contentious. Moreover, different people have different expectations of dictionaries. Language scholars, for example, have different expectations from members of the general public, even that part of the public that is well informed on language matters. As we will see from what happened when *Webster's Third* was published in 1961, fierce controversy can erupt

17

when the expectations that many influential people have of dictionaries are not met. One consequence is that the public for whom dictionaries are produced remains no wiser about either language matters in general or words in particular.

Popular concern with words often ascribes a certain magic and power to them. Are there words in the language we should be protected from because they will corrupt us or, if not us, our children? Periodically, books are banned because of their "dirty words," or there is some kind of organized protest. For example, in the early 1990s, the BBC met with criticism over reading *Lady Chatterley's Lover* on the air. Evidently, at the end of the twentieth century many people are not ready to see in print or hear on the air words that we know exist and cannot escape from hearing, but which are deemed offensive because they are so simple and forthright.

Newspapers like the *Globe and Mail* are particularly coy in this matter. They may be papers with considerable pretensions, yet they insist on not reporting the so-called four-letter words, preferring instead to use dashes or say something like *expletive deleted*. What should we make of this? In order to understand what is being said, we must know the word that is not printed and those who produce such newspapers know that. They know we know what is there but they are not going to print it. Why? Because they will get irate letters from "Concerned" and "Disgusted"? Because they will be validating a certain kind of language? Because they will be corrupting their readers? Because they are protecting the language? We know that people very quickly comment when such words are eventually included in a dictionary. They obviously went looking for them so they must know them. (When a woman complimented Samuel Johnson for not including such words in his dictionary, he remarked that she could know that only if she had searched for them.)

Avoiding contact with certain words may be something like trying to avoid a disease like cholera by trying not to think about it rather than by taking sensible precautions. A classic example of this phenomenon occurred near the end of 1990 when for several months the Canadian Minister of Finance refused to mention what he called the *r-* word, i.e., *recession*. Do not mention the word and the event will not happen. He was unsuccessful and there was a recession. However, I suspect that this kind of avoidance behavior is universal not national, this belief that there is a special reality to words, that they are more than signs, and that we must treat them reverentially or they will rise up and overwhelm us. To the unthinkable and the uneatable we must add the unspeakable, all evidence of the way in which culture both guides and constrains our behavior.

5 A Largely Grammarless Language

When we read books on language, we sometimes encounter statements like the following from Richard Grant White's *Words and Their Uses*: English is "a grammarless tongue" and "words are formed into sentences by the operation of an invisible power, which is like magnetism." In his 1880 book *Every-day English* White also tells us in his Preface that: "English has with some trifling exceptions no grammatical construction," and later we find out why this is so: "The reason . . . why English has no grammar is that it is unencumbered with cases, genders, moods, and tenses and, we may almost say, with grammatical person. For these are the essences of grammar, or rather, I should say, its conditions; without them there can be no grammar." According to White, English did have a grammar once, but it has ceased to have one. These sentiments are not unlike those expressed more recently by Philip Howard in *The State of the Language*. Howard tells us that English grammar "is becoming progressively simpler," a statement unaccompanied by a single bit of supporting evidence.

In another book, *The Language Bar*, Victor Grove declares that English has "a highly advanced and simplified grammar, which demands a great deal of ingenuity and intelligence." Later, he assures us that English is "a largely grammarless language," but as he has already told us that "it is far more difficult for an English person to learn English than, for instance, it is for a Frenchman to learn French or a German to learn German," we must ask ourselves why this should be so if English is lacking in grammar. Grove informs us that: "Chinese has gone furthest in the direction of simplification and abbreviation, so far further, indeed, that to-day the term grammar can hardly be applied to it any more," and later still adds that: "Chinese . . . has preserved only the mere rudiments of something that hardly deserves the name of grammar, and yet it would be ludicrous to say that a Chinese cannot fully understand his language unless he has studied a highly grammatical language like Greek, Russian, or Hebrew." At last we find the clue that unravels this puzzle: grammar is something that certain languages have and others do not.

Do some languages have grammars and others not? For example, do those languages that we can describe, however uncomfortably, in terms we have inherited from Greek and Latin, have grammars and those that we cannot describe in this way do not? But what would a "grammarless language" be like? Like Chinese, of course. But Chinese has a grammar and so does every language in the world. A grammar of a language is the particular set of rules that speakers of that language follow when they communicate with each other. Every language has a grammar whether or not someone has tried to figure out what the rules are or describe them in writing. Moreover, its grammar is unique; that is why English is English and Chinese is Chinese. A grammarless language is a contradiction. There would be no possibility of communicating with others; there would be no English language and no Chinese language.

It is often asserted that if we know the grammar of our language in the sense of having been schooled to talk about the structure of that language, we will use it better. Traditionally, a Latinate model of description is preferred. Many might agree with Samuel Kirkham when he declared in *English Grammar in Familiar Lectures* first published in 1829 that: "Without the knowledge and application of grammar rules, it is impossible for any one to think, speak, read, or write with accuracy." This statement is false if Kirkham is referring to conscious knowledge of the grammar of a language. What he is referring to is the importance – to him at least – of Latin or of a Latin-based grammar of English in "training the mind." Many have shared and continue to share this view, one that has been the basis of centuries of education in the West. A strong Latinate tradition exists and continues to influence how we talk about language, e.g., in how we talk about the various parts of speech. However, it may not be a very useful tradition.

Does the study of the grammar of a language help a person to think better? Does it improve the mind? Does it make us more logical and allow us to turn that logic on language itself in order to improve the language and correct any faults it may have? Does it require us to use the superior knowledge we have gained in doing this to improve others' use of language? Many would answer "yes" to all these questions.

A considerable confusion exists about what we mean by the word *grammar* itself. Do we mean the rules and principles that people actually are following when they speak a language? Or should a grammar be a set of statements of rules and principles that tells people how they should be using their language? The rules and principles would be different in the two cases.

Rules and principles are important when we consider language issues, but more important is how people decide to go about determining them. Paul Johnson, the well-known critic and writer, missed more that one point when, in comparing English to French, he wrote in the *Times Educational Supplement* in 1986 that: "Of course, French is an easier language to spell and write – and indeed pronounce – once you know the rules." What are the rules Johnson refers to so casually, what does it mean to know them, and how do we measure what is "easier" and what is more difficult in a language? These are all serious questions but Johnson fails to address a single one of them. English children speak English and therefore in a very important sense "know" the rules of English; likewise French-speaking children "know" the rules of French. There is no reason to assume that French children find the task of pronouncing French more or less onerous than English children find the task of pronouncing English.

Johnson is not alone in holding such views. The terms *grammar* and *rule* are part of the vocabulary we use for talking about language. We cannot escape them. We are confronted everyday with having to decide exactly what they cover. How should a person react on hearing *It couldn't be a more perfect day for this year's parade?* with its joining of *more* to *perfect*? We hear and say *Put your best foot forward,* but there is no discussion of *best* used in that context – we have only two feet! However, there are serious discusions focusing on *between–among, each other–one another*, and *either . . . or*. Who should we turn to for advice in matters of grammar and rules? (Or should that be *Whom should we turn to?* or even *To whom should we turn?*, and, if so, why?)

6 Is British English Effete?

Many of us readily make judgments about others on the basis of language alone. Speaking one language rather than another may get you into severe trouble in certain parts of the world. It may cost you your life, as it did once for those who failed the *shibboleth* test. Today the penalties are usually not so severe but they can still be quite exacting.

Within a language one of its varieties may carry considerably more prestige than another. Greeks and Norwegians can rouse themselves to great passions over the two distinct varieties each language has. Which true Brit has gone on record as praising the introduction of Americanisms into the British variety of English? Which red-blooded American does not regard the Oxbridge variety of English as somehow effete (while possibly admitting at the same time that it does have a certain distinction about it)? Who praises the language of working-class Birmingham or Glasgow? Who rates highly the language of rural Newfoundland or Jersey City? Which native of France asserts the superiority of non-Parisian French to the Parisian variety? Or, more unthinkable, of English to French? And why should how a speaker says something often be regarded more critically than the actual content of what the speaker says, considerations of form sometimes preempting considerations of content?

We know that people's attitudes toward a speaker can differ according to the accent the speaker adopts. Recent evidence from the United Kingdom suggests that those with regional accents are often judged to be sincere whereas those with some variety of prestige accent are regarded less favorably. These same prestige accents lend those who use them an authority and competence that those using the non-prestige accents do not find themselves credited with. The consequence is a paradox: those who sound competent and powerful are not always to be trusted, and those you might be inclined to trust you may regard as neither competent nor powerful. Perhaps that is just a lesson of history! Prestigious varieties of languages have long been promoted through formal education and the media; why do so many people continue to resist them and continue to find comfort and solidarity in other varieties?

Such phenomena are not confined to English and those who speak English. If we ask a speakers of Arabic, a language of many dialects, who speaks the best Arabic, we will almost certainly be told that those who speak like the person asked do so, although there may be a grudging admission that perhaps the Bedouins have a claim too. The reason is that whereas Arabic has a standard written variety based on the Qur'an, it has poorly standardized local varieties and no Arab is about to concede inferiority in language to another Arab. Furthermore, we will be told that Arabic itself is more beautiful than any other language, being both logically and symmetrically structured. It is after all an Islamic belief that God chose Arabic to speak to Mohammad. Christian Arabs have even gone so far as to declare that the Bible is "better" in Arabic than in any other language. However, if Arabic is so beautiful and logical, where does that leave French and all we have heard about it from the French themselves?

7 Belief Versus Reality

Why do people hold the beliefs they hold about language? What are the origins of these beliefs? What are the consequences? To a serious student of language many such beliefs appear to be bizarre. However, we cannot ignore them if we want to understand how language functions in society. Part of a person's knowledge of language is a set of beliefs about that language and possibly about other languages too. Like Caliban, we learn a lot more than words when we learn a language. Much of what we are taught about language should come labeled with a warning that it could be bad for our linguistic health. Unfortunately, if it did come so labeled, most of us would lack the ability to understand what we are being told so accustomed are we to other views of the sickness and health of our language.

Linguists have their own beliefs about language. What is remarkable is the gap between these two sets of beliefs, the beliefs that linguists hold about language and the beliefs that most others hold. In a 1948 paper entitled "Secondary and Tertiary Responses to Language" Leonard Bloomfield, one of the founders of modern linguistics, described how someone is likely to approach a linguist: that person "first alleges ignorance and alludes modestly to the status of his own speech, but then advances the traditional lore in a fully authoritative tone." Bloomfield added that such a person also seems to get a lot of pleasure out of doing this.

Linguists themselves must carry some of the responsibility for being treated like this. Most have simply abandoned the task of trying to inform the public about what they do, preferring the pleasures of "linguistic theory" to the perils of language education and writing for each other to writing for public consumption. In the absence of informed opinion, popular views of language abound, assume importance, and have consequences. None of us is free of them, for even if we do not share these views we are still subject to them as others act in accordance with them. I suspect that much public discussion of language will continue to be dominated by irrational and emotional arguments presented under the guise of reason, logic, and common sense.

Language
and Belief

When we read about language and listen to people discuss language issues, we encounter a wide variety of views on almost every topic that is mentioned. It may be useful, therefore, to look closely at some of these views about language, for example, ideas about the possible origins of language, the purpose it serves in human existence, and its nature. We might look at opinions concerning whether a language is essentially something spoken or something written, and at the virtues claimed for some languages and therefore the shortcomings ascribed to others. We will find many different opinions expressed; we may encounter a few interesting facts. What we will certainly discover is that opinions will far outnumber facts, but these opinions will be no less influential for that. We will find that many discussions of language proceed quite nicely without any evidence at all for the views that are expressed. Normal rational modes of inquiry seem to be blocked; it is as though learning a language prevents us from understanding just what we have done in that learning and are doing when we listen, speak, read, and write.

1 "Poohpooh," "Bowwow," and "Dingdong"

A number of vague, superficially intriguing ideas concerning how it is that human beings have language but other species do not have been discussed from time immemorial. Many involve the belief that language is a human invention, something like the wheel. The reasons given for this invention differ. One theory, sometimes called the "poohpooh" theory, is that language originated from the expression of the emotions. For example, in *Essai sur l'origine des langues*, Jean-Jacques Rousseau, the eighteenth-century French philosopher, rejected necessity alone as being an adequate reason for the origin of language. He preferred to believe that it had originated to express the passions of love, hate, anger, and joy. Another account, the "bowwow" theory, holds that the origins of language are to be found in human imitation of sounds in the environment. A variation of this theory, the "dingdong" theory, maintains that human resonance to substances in the environment provides the explanation. In his *Traité de la formation mécanique des langues et des principes physiques de l'étymologie* of 1765, Charles de Brosses, President of the *parlement de Dijon*, declared that "hollow" sounds had originally been used for hollow objects, and that words beginning with *st-* were developed for things that were firm or steadfast and those beginning with *fl-* for things that were floating or liquid.

The "tata" theory finds the origins of language lie in human gesturing. This theory is associated with Étienne Bonnot de Condillac, another eighteenth-century *philosophe*, who declared that: *"Tous les sentiments de l'âme peuvent être exprimés par les attitudes du corps"* (All the feelings of the soul can be expressed by bodily gestures). The "yoheho" theory says the human need for companionship was all important. Rousseau, who was not entirely consistent in his views about the origins of language, also mentioned in his essay on the origin of language that the companionship of mother and child must have been particularly important as must have been that required to dig wells. Finally, the "tararaboomdeay" theory ascribes the origins to an underlying human need to ritualize activity.

These are all intriguing theories but debating them is pointless. None is scientifically disprovable: we cannot do anything to test them. Moreover, none is based on any realistic idea of what language is like, particularly of its complexity and of its relationship to the development of our species.

The basic dispute concerning the origins of language has always been between those who think language is a human invention and those who regard it as a natural phenomenon, possibly the gift of a beneficent deity. In *Cratylus* Plato has Cratylus tell us that language mirrors the world; however, Homogenes says language is arbitrary and Socrates offers a compromise. Here we see the "naturalists," those who believe that language is either a divine gift or a natural, human endowment, pitted against the "conventionalists," those who believe that language is a human invention. If it is natural, we cannot do much about it in the way of improvement because it is what it is. If, on the other hand, it is conventional, we can "improve" it. Aristotle was a conventionalist and, as we well know, his thought has had an important influence on western intellectual life. Plato, the realist, has been much less influential.

Most people believe that language is a uniquely human attribute. Isocrates, the rhetorician and teacher and contemporary of Plato, argued that it was language *logos* that separated humans from animals and allowed humans to reason. But is that human attribute a divine gift? This is a widely held belief. We can even be like Johann Gottfried Herder, the German philosopher, and regard language as a divine gift but one that humans should feel free to develop to suit their various purposes or like the jurist and anthropologist Lord Monboddo, who in his *Of the Origin and Progress of Language*, published in six volumes between 1773 and 1792, declared that the only thing that distinguished humans from orangutans was the fact that humans had been blessed with language whereas orangutans had not. Such ideas prompted Samuel Johnson to observe that: "Monboddo does not know he is talking nonsense" and that his conjectures were "idle." "Nonsense" and "idle" these ideas may have been to Johnson two centuries ago, but similar ideas are found today. Do chimpanzees share our language ability? Or is language unique to humans?

2 Before Babel

Was there an original language and, if there was, what was it like? There has been much speculation on this topic. Rousseau's position in his *Émile* of 1762 was that although there must have been an original language, it was eventually forgotten. How good was it? Was it a very limited language? Did it express a few sensations, contain a few words that served as names for objects in the immediate environment, and possibly require accompanying gestures in order to be fully intelligible? Or was it perfect from the very beginning? The Scottish philosopher and rhetorician James Beattie averred in his *Theory of Language* of 1788 that "the first language, whatever it was, must . . . have been perfect." Noah Webster in his *American Dictionary of the English Language* of 1828, on the other hand, thought that although it might have been perfect in the beginning, it probably was not very "copious." Moreover, it had certainly ceased to exist. But what evidence is there for either view? Such claims as these led the Linguistic Society of Paris founded in 1866 to prohibit in its second bylaw the reading of papers on the origins of language. The society had decided that nothing useful, in the sense of being scientific, could be said on the topic. But that action has not prevented continued speculation.

The biblical story of Adam giving names is well-known. Genesis 2, 19 tells us that "whatsoever Adam called every living creature, that was the name thereof." Even before this, Genesis 1: 3 informs us that "God said, 'Let there be light,' and there was light." (The name Adam itself comes from the word for the dust out of which Adam was created.) Such accounts have considerable influence today among those who believe that biblical accounts of anything must be accepted at face value. In such a view the Tower of Babel story in Genesis 11: 6–9 neatly takes care of the variety of languages we have in the world – and makes a moral issue of it at the same time! In *The Annals of the World* of 1658, James Ussher, Archbishop of Armagh, pinpointed the very moment of creation and therefore of the creation of language, offering noon, October 23, 4004 BCE as a precise time and date. Long before Ussher St Augustine in the fourth century declared that Adam and Eve had spoken Hebrew in Paradise. Another variation of the story told in Genesis is attributed to Andreas Kempe in *The Languages of Paradise*, published in German in Hamburg. Kempe, who was being satirical at the time, informs us that in the Garden of Eden God spoke Swedish, Adam spoke Danish, and the serpent spoke French, a claim that tells us more about seventeenth-century Scandinavian–French relationships than it does about the origins of language.

Has the original language disappeared completely? Is it discoverable? According to the Greek historian Herodotus, Psammetichus of Egypt conducted an experiment in which he isolated two children in order to find out what language humans would speak "naturally." He decided that this language was Phrygian because the children's first word was determined to be *bekos*, the Phrygian word for bread. Others who repeated this experiment, like Frederick II of Germany, James IV of Scotland, and a Moghul emperor by the name of Akbar Khan, got different results, but predictably so.

Hebrew has been widely regarded as the original language. Dante Alighieri, the great Italian poet, said as much well over six centuries ago when he wrote *De vulgari eloquentia*; however, by the time he wrote *Paradisio* he had changed his mind, proclaiming there that Hebrew was a human creation. He was also of the opinion that the angels in heaven read each other's thoughts directly without the need for language at all! In his *Mithridates* of 1555 Conrad Gesner said that Hebrew was the original language and its words would be found, though badly corrupted, in the languages his book surveyed. Samuel Butler was another who believed that Hebrew was the original language, declaring in *English Grammar* in 1633 that: "The Hebrew . . . [is] the language of our great Grandfather Adam, which, untill the Confusion, all people of the earth did speak." Other languages for which original-language status has been claimed are Greek, Phoenician, Chaldee, Swedish, and something called Teutonic, the dialect of Antwerp, the latter according to a Dutchman Goropius Becanus (or Jan van Gorp) in the late sixteenth century. Even Chinese gets into the list. In *An Historical Essay endeavouring the Probability that the Language of the Empire of China is the Primitive Language* of 1699 John Webb expressed the opinion that Noah had found his way to China after the Great Flood and that Chinese was the original language because it had escaped the linguistic confusion that followed the destruction of the Tower of Babel.

The view that Hebrew is the original language persists. For a brief while the bookstore at the University of Toronto had on its shelves a newly published book that claimed to demonstrate how English was derived from Hebrew, the original language. A glance at its contents showed the evidence to be bizarre, but since the book disappeared quickly, someone must have been impressed with its claims. Bizarre accounts of the histories of languages and words are not unusual. For example, there are accounts of Italian that trace it through Etruscan, then Greek, and finally to the "original" Hebrew. Poisinet de Sivry claimed in *Origines des premières sociétés* of 1770 that Celtic is the original language because so many words in different languages are of Celtic origin. There is a Basque claim, dating back at least to the sixteenth century, that Basque is the original language. In 1815 Erro y Aspiroz argued in *El Mundo Primitivo* that Basque had certain characteristics that an original language must have had: it was euphonious and exhibited the principle of least effort. Like the recent book with its claim for Hebrew all such assertions rest on complete distortions of historical facts, principally bizarre etymologizing. The goal is always the glorification of a language and its speakers any cost. Perhaps Jonathan Swift made the most telling comment on such work in his *A Discourse to Prove the Antiquity of the English Tongue* of 1765. In this work Swift neatly reverses the whole procedure and uses the same bizarre – and sometimes quite ribald – etymologizing to derive Hebrew, Greek, and Latin from English and prove that English was at that time exactly 2,634 years old!

Although people might not be tempted to claim that the language they speak is the original one, they are far less hesitant about claiming that it is "older" than some other language or languages. "Older" generally means "better" too! Such claims make little or no sense. We must assume that all languages have an ancestry and are like people in that respect. Moreover, like people the ancestry of some is better known than the ancestry of others, and some people are more concerned than others about their ancestry, e.g., aristocrats, descendants of passengers on the Mayflower, Mormons, etc. Each individual's ancestry goes as far back as the ancestry of any king, queen, president, or pope. Languages are like people in this respect; they all have histories but these histories are not always readily or easily available. Furthermore, just like the ancestry of individuals, the ancestry of languages can be traced back only so far with any degree of confidence.

3 Produced by Necessity

Opposed to the idea that language is a gift from a beneficent deity is the idea that language is a human creation, and, like all human creations, is therefore subject to change and possibly "improvement." Any such improvement might lead those who use the improved variety to think better and produce a better world. This view puts humans firmly within the natural world. It requires that they try to understand that world and their place in it.

In the seventeenth century the Port-Royal grammarians of France treated language as a human creation. For example, Antoine Arnauld and Claude Lancelot in their *Grammaire générale et raisonnée* of 1660 said as much; they emphasized the connection between language and human reasoning. They believed that the surface irregularities of languages concealed underlying regularities. This belief in a connection between reason and language was to find echoes in later work, e.g., in Gottfried Wilhelm Leibniz's *New Essays Concerning Human Understanding*, in which he argued that humans had created language in order to be understood and to reason.

The eighteenth-century *philosophes*, a distinguished group of French philosophers and writers committed to the pursuit of reason, felt that there had to be a reason for the existence of language. Thinkers such as Étienne Bonnot de Condillac in *Essai sur l'origine des connoissances humaines* of 1746, Jean-le-Rond D'Alembert, Antoine Court de Gebelin, and still later Voltaire debated its origins. They decided that language had probably been created on many different occasions, and Voltaire went so far as to claim in his *Dictionnaire philosophique* that each species has its own language. The *philosophes* also debated the nature of language and how it could be improved.

None of these views opposes the notion the language is innate in humans. The *philosophes* believed that language is an innate, human capacity. This innateness reveals itself in the actual languages humans have devised for themselves, and, since these are human creations, they could and should be improved. In England, Samuel Johnson also acknowledged in 1747 in the Plan for the dictionary that he was eventually to compile that humans had created language: "It did not descend to us in a state of uniformity and perfection, but was produced by necessity and enlarged by accident, and is therefore composed of dissimilar parts, thrown together by negligence, by affectation, by learning, or by ignorance." It could be improved – and if it could be, it should be! If it could be improved, who should improve it and what exactly is an improvement? Aye, there's the rub!

4 Towards . . . a Philosophical Language

In his much celebrated *Novum Organum* of 1620 Francis Bacon dealt with the inadequacies of language as a vehicle for thought. Bacon claimed that language limits our abilty to reason rather than that reason limits our ability to use language. Later, John Locke devoted the third volume of *An Essay concerning Human Understanding* to a discussion of the inadequacies of language: its imprecision and inconsistencies; the difficulty, if not sheer impossibility, of translation; and the problems that constant change brings about. Locke believed that words are the signs or marks of ideas in the mind.

Locke's view about the difficulties of translation between languages contrasts with the view that the theologian John Calvin had expressed a century before. Calvin marveled that people speaking different languages could communicate with one another and achieve understanding, in this case religious understanding. His conclusion was not a linguistic one: it was that this fact testified to a capacity for human redemption.

According to Locke's contemporary Leibniz, it was the human desire to be understood that led to the development of language. In *New Essays Concerning Human Understanding*, written between 1700 and 1705, Leibniz pointed out that along with language came the power to reason. The various languages in existence had themselves descended from a single, original language.

Once we abandon the idea that we can recover the original language and are convinced that we must take language as we find it and try to make it better, we can entertain a variety of possibilities. We may decide to start again as it were and invent the perfect language. Condillac believed that the success that had been achieved in mathemetics could serve as a model for such a language, which might then usefully be adopted throughout the world. Numerous attempts were made to construct a suitable language, e.g., by the French mathematician and philosopher Descartes, by Leibniz, and by John Wilkins, one of the founders of the Royal Society, who, in *Essay Towards a Real Character and a Philosophical Language* of 1668, tried to construct a language based on reason that would be suitable for science.

In a similar attempt James Harris published *Hermes, or A Philosophical Enquiry concerning Universal Grammar* in 1751. Harris believed that there was a universal reason and also something that he called "ONE TRUTH." He declared that there was a "GRAMMAR UNIVERSAL," which he defined as "that Grammar, which without regarding the several Idioms of particular Languages, only respects those principles that are essential to them all." This view, rather interestingly for the time, recognized that Latin has certain deficiencies. Jean Baptiste de la Chappelle, writing in *L'art de communiquer ses idées* in 1763, also admitted that Latin had some deficiencies but, nevertheless, thought that it could be developed to serve the purpose of a universal language. In each case the concern is with trying to find a language that best gives expression to human reasoning. The general problem is an age-old one: do people need language to reason or do they need reason to use language? It is another version of the classic chicken-and-egg conundrum. Herder found reason and language inseparable. He said so in his 1772 prize-winning essay on the origin of language, declaring that they had originated and developed together and were completely interdependent.

A further issue concerns the relationship of language to logic and of logic to language. How logical are languages? Do they have their own logic? In *Mankind, Nation, and Individual from a Linguistic Point of View* of 1925, the Danish linguist Otto Jespersen wrote that he could not entirely agree that "language has nothing to do with logic," because we often do try to be logical when we use language. He added that what many people describe as the logic of English grammar is just those resemblances to Latin that they believe should hold, e.g., the argument for *It is I* being somehow "more logical" that *It is me*.

We can see the dilemma here. A sign in a store reads as follows: *The best lowest prices in Toronto.* Is the sign illogical because of the two superlative adjectives? Or is it ungrammatical? Or is it a problem of redundancy? Whatever the answer, the meaning of the sign is clear, just as the meaning of *I didn't do nothing* is clear. The use of *hisself* for *himself* is also logical if the model for reference is *herself*, and so is the use of *it's* for *its*, if the model is *John's*. Logic is not a foolproof test by any means, because it is essentially a matter of whose logic we are to follow.

A few moments of serious thought should allow us to dismisss most arguments that languages are or should be logical. When, in Lewis Carroll's *Alice Through the Looking-Glass*, the Messenger protests to the King that: "I'm sure nobody walks much faster than I do!" and the King replies: "He can't do that or else he'd have been here first," we see logic and language working against each other. Languages are naturally occurring phenomena. They are what they are. On the other hand, logic is a human invention and there is no reason to believe that humans can reshape languages in any significant way by trying to make them mirror that invention But that does not stop them from trying to do so.

5 Words, Words, Words

Much discussion about language turns on issues having to do with words. For many of us languages are just large collections of words. Many people believe that words have fixed meanings and that a knowledge of English is equivalent to a knowledge of the vocabulary of English. If they want to learn another language, then all they must do is find the equivalent words in that language for the English words they already know. The language sections of bookstores are full of books that reinforce this belief.

The belief that words are ultimately of divine origin and that they are names is behind Adam's naming role in Genesis. In the New Testament the book of John also begins: "In the beginning was the Word." The earliest linguistic debate in western literature is in Plato's *Cratylus* and is about the correctness of names, in particular whether or not Hermogenes is correctly named. A considerable part of western philosophy is a continuation of this traditional focus on what words mean and how words relate to objects. This tradition has thoroughly influenced not only the whole history of language study but also how westerners have thought about language.

Jonathan Swift satirized the obsession people have with words in his *Gulliver's Travels*. He describes the members of the grand academy of Logado, "sages" who were so obsessed that names (or words) should be used correctly that they carried around with them large bundles of objects with which to "converse" in order to ensure that there would be no misunderstanding. The results are ludicrous, and Swift tells us that "women in conjunction with the vulgar and illiterate," these "constant irreconcilable enemies to science," as he puts it, objected to such practices. Of course, it is the false science of the sages that is really under attack.

Every day we see similar concerns expressed about whether certain words are being used "properly." We see concerns with the magical powers of words and with avoiding certain words. We find mystical powers attributed to words and names: "In the name of the Father, the Son, and the Holy Spirit." We observe a similar phenomenon in the renaming of kings, emperors, and popes, and of movie stars, pop singers, and even writers. Personal names are often assigned with very great care. Certain names are avoided. And there are those stories about the power that knowing a particular name may confer, e.g., Rumpelstiltskin. Many words have their own very strong reality to those who use them; their users cannot easily separate the words from their referents.

Consequently, what words "really mean" and who gets to decide that can become important issues. Humpty Dumpty sums up this situation neatly in *Alice Through the Looking-Glass* when he says: "When *I* use a word it means just what I choose it to mean – neither more nor less." Alice objects: "The question is whether you *can* make words mean so many different things." Humpty Dumpty's reply settles the issue: "The question is which is to be master – that's all." Where do we find the "true meanings" of words? Who indeed shall be master?

The *philosophe* Claude-Adrian Helvetius was interested in "*la vraie signification des mots*" (the true meaning of words) but did little more than speculate on the matter. Others have been interested in the "correct use" of words, which is a different issue but a very important one. Perhaps a clue to either or both concerns lies in etymology, the history of words. Until the Renaissance, however, etymology meant the study of the true meanings of words not a description of their historical origins, and we still find traces of this approach. Etymology was also a bizarre pursuit but, bizarreness has never been missing in speculations about language. For example, it was possible for disputants in ancient Rome to argue that Latin *homo* (man) originated from *humus* (earth) because of man's earthly, non-divine origin and at the same time derive *lutum* (mud) from *lavare* (wash) because it was an opposite and *lucus* (grove) from *lucere* (shine) because light did not shine there!

There is much more to a language than words. Each language has its own grammar and sounds. Its words, however these are defined, are quite different from those of any other language. Furthermore, all these various bits and pieces fit together in an intricate arrangement which changes over time and varies over space. However, a strong belief persists that language is just words because the study of words and concerns about words have become central to our thinking about language.

Even some of those who are most sophisticated in language and literary matters are beguiled by words. George Steiner, writing of the Kabbalah in *After Babel*, says that it "records the conjecture, no doubt heretical, that there shall come a day when translation is not only unnecessary but inconceivable. Words will rebel against man. They will shake off the servitude of meaning. They will 'become only themselves, and as dead stones in our mouths' . . . men and women will have been freed forever from the burden and the slendour of the ruin of Babel. But which, one wonders, will be the greater silence?" I do not know what this

Language and Belief

passage means: words rebelling against man; words shaking off the servitude of meaning; and so on. Here words lose any meaning they might have under the weight of Steiner's rhetoric. Meaningful discussions of language matters cannot be conducted in this way.

6 The First Word and the Last Word

Because words are so important to us, parents are likely to make much of what they believe to be a child's "first word." They are likely to believe that the child then continues to add words to this first word and learns the language in this way. It helps if we believe that children are good imitators of adults. Voltaire so believed, informing us in his *Dictionnaire philosophique* that: "*L'expérience nous apprend que les enfants ne sont qu'imitateurs*" (Experience teaches us that children are only imitators). We may want to go further and consider, as Psammetichus and others did, although not in the way they did it, that we can learn something about the origins of language in the species through the study of how children acquire language. Lord Monboddo, for example, thought that a study of children's language, the language behavior of the deaf, and the languages of "primitive" peoples might offer clues to the ultimate origins of language.

There is much that is misguided about such beliefs. They do not concern themselves with very basic issues and are replete with false assumptions. For example, what is important about language is the total system – grammar if you will – of sounds and meanings that lies behind the words. How might such a system be acquired? We know that it is far too complex to be acquired through imitation alone or through any kind of process that we usually describe as conscious learning. Language seems to be innate in humans, a biological given. Learning a language is much more like learning to walk than it is like learning to play chess.

The human species has evolved over millions of years and language is a relatively recent phenomenon. The current view is that language is as old as our particular variety of that species; we are what we are because we have language. In this view a change occurred in the brain structure of our ancestors perhaps some 200,000 years ago, a change that rapidly introduced language as we know it into the world. According to Derek Bickerton in *Language and Species*, before that time there may have been some rudimentary form of communication among the ancestors of those in whom this change occurred. Somewhat speculatively, Bickerton uses the language of very young children, a maltreated girl Genie, who was locked up during childhood and deprived of any kind of language use, of pidgin languages, and of attempts to teach human language to apes in order to demonstrate what this forerunner of human language might have been like. However, language as we know it today is qualitatively different from any rudimentary language. It is also not just words. Nor was it invented.

7 The Mystery of Writing

Not only language but writing itself has been given a divine origin as a gift. According to I. J. Gelb in *A Study in Writing*, the deity varied; for Mesopotamians it was the goddess Nisaba, for Babylonians the god Nabû, for Egyptians the god Thoth, for Muslims God, for Hindus Brahma, for Chinese either Fohi or Ts'ang Chien, and for Irish a mythical Ogmios. The Cyrillic alphabet of St Cyril of the ninth century was believed to be divinely inspired. In each case a special group claimed this divine connection for itself for some purpose. For example, the Cyrillic alphabet gave Old Church Slavonic and the variety of Christianity associated with it a much needed boost at the time the claim was made.

We find writing associated with magic. The original meaning of the word *grammar* has to do with writing and, by extension, book-learning. This learning also became associated with the occult. It led to the development of another variant of the word *glamor* with its meaning of "spell-casting power," a meaning found today to some extent in a phrase like *glamor girl*. There is the example from ancient Greece of the effect of the writings of Pythagoras none of which have survived. We know from reports and comments by his followers that many Greeks saw something mystical in what Pythagoras wrote and taught; he was apparently the first person to grasp the idea that it might be possible to express characteristics of the real world in mathematical terms.

There are other examples. We find inscriptions on houses to ward off evil. There is the practice of carrying objects with certain words or texts written on them, or pages from a religious book. Some people practice cabalistic rites. Tibetan monks may spend hours writing words on objects, even on water. A particularly interesting belief system attributable to the magic of the written word is the "cargo cult" system found in Melanesia in which the written artefacts of language play a key role. On the other hand, there may be a social prohibition on the translation of certain books, e.g., the Qur'an, or outright censorship and book burning, the consequences of thinking that certain written words must be proscribed.

Writing is a human invention and the various writing systems represent speech in one way or another. Aristotle said that "written words are the signs of words spoken" and agreed with Plato on that point at least. The earliest writing seems to have served as a memory device for speaking, but gradually writing developed a life of its own, a life which misleads many people. As linguists constantly remind us, writing is a way of recording language and is not itself language.

Writing is a way of recording language with its own conventions and its own possibilities. It is not *just* a way of recording language. It records a different kind of language from the spoken language, e.g., the language of logic, mathematics, and computers. It creates possibilities for using language in special ways, e.g., the possibilities that follow from being able to see a form of language. Some very simple everyday uses show us the difference, e.g., the language used in labels or menus, or the language of newspaper headlines. No-one would ever say something like *served with a generous portion of garden-fresh peas cooked in a creamy butter*. The headline *PRINCE WEDS STARLET* has not only its own grammatical rules, i.e. no *a* or *the* in front of *starlet*, but also its own special verb, because *wed* seems to be used only by those who write headlines.

Linguists have sometimes been accused of overstating the case

39

that the spoken language is primary and that writing is a secondary representation of the spoken language. There is some justification for this criticism. However, there is no justification at all for believing that we derive the spoken language from the written language or that the written language should guide us in the use of the spoken language, views that clearly puts the cart before the horse.

8 Plato Walks with the Macedonian Swineherd

Another commonly held belief is that some languages are "primitive" while others are "advanced." Furthermore, some people claim that the study of "primitive languages" and "primitive peoples" might bring us a better understanding of the evolution of both language and human culture. We might, for example, try to see what kinds of words and concepts are missing from such languages. We hear from time to time statements such as a certain language lacks a word for a particular concept or that its speakers have no concept of "time." A language may not have words for particular concepts because such concepts are irrelevant to the users of that language. Not long ago English had no words for discussing nuclear physics and computers, but it developed the words that were necessary as the users of the languge began to pursue certain interests. There is no reason to suppose that any language lacks the means to develop ways of talking about anything that becomes important to its users.

There are no such things as primitive languages. Voltaire's words on the subject in an article in his *Dictionnaire philosophique* are quite appropriate: *"Il n'y a pas eu plus de langue primitive et d'alphabet primitif que de chêne primitif et que d'herbe primitive"* (A primitive language or a primitive alphabet has no more existed than a primitive oak or a primitive grass). The one possible exception is pidgin languages but these are never the first languages of those who use them; they are supplementary languages with very restricted uses. As for the idea that a language may lack the concept of time, the observation means no more than that the people who speak that language do not share the observer's concept of time. Why should they? Anthropologists are also quick to point out that so-called "primitive peoples" have extraordinarily complex cultures.

The term *primitive* when used for language and culture is highly pejorative. The term *barbarian* had similar strong pejorative beginnings. The Greeks called all those who did not speak Greek barbarians; they were the unintelligibles, and to a Greek to be unintelligible was to be inferior. This use of the term has persisted. We find, for example, in 1712 the *Spectator* describing the Hottentots as: "Barbarians . . . having no language among them but a confused Gabble, which is neither well understood by themselves or others." Well understood by others they may not have been and for a variety of reasons, but they most certainly understood one another, and it was no gabble they were using!

There is no reason either to believe Noah Webster's words in the Appendix to his *Dissertations on the English Language* in 1789 that: "As savages proceed in forming languages, they lose the guttural sounds, in some measure, and adopt the use of labials, and the more open vowels. The ease of speaking facilitates this progress, and the pronunciation of words is softened, in proportion to a national refinement of manners." Webster thought that this principle also showed the superiority of French, Spanish, and Italian to German! There is no possibility of associating certain sounds with less "refined" languages peoples and others with more "refined" ones. Sounds just do not distribute across languages according to such a principle: there is no such principle.

All languages appear to be equally complex. As Edward Sapir, often paired with Leonard Bloomfield as the one of the founders of linguistic studies in North America, wrote in *Language*, "When it comes to linguistic form, Plato walks with the Macedonian swineherd, Confucius with the head-hunting savage of Assam." The only possible fault with that statement is the use of the word *savage*. It is doubtful that we can learn anything at all about the evolution of language from some primitive form of language by studying any of the existing languages in the world. The only exception to this statement might be trying to find out how pidgin languages become creolized, but even this approach to the issue of language origins seems highly dubious.

41

We might do a little better by looking closely at cultures that differ widely from those in which we were brought up, but here ideas about progress can get in the way. Just as our predecessors looked at other languages and cultures to try to find out what the past was like so that they could compare it to the present in the hope of predicting the future, we do the same. After many centuries of looking back to golden ages from which there had been various kinds of decline, including language decline, thinkers from the eighteenth century on have generally regarded change as progress and improvement, with language being a notable exception.

Some people assume that a language will prosper only if they personally take charge of its care and protection and succeed in getting the great unwashed to follow. If they do not do this, the language will remain imperfect and possibly regress. Consequently, definite action is called for, because, as Denis Diderot, still another *philosophe* and the chief editor of the famous *Encyclopédie*, declared, *"il faut qu'elle [une nation] reste ignorante et presque barbare* [that word again!] *tant que sa langue est imparfaite"* (a nation must remain ignorant and almost barbarous so long as its language is imperfect).

The most sensible view about any language is that it changes. It neither regresses nor progresses. It is in many respects the same as all other languages but in a few unique. A sensible approach would be one that explores such issues and examines the various consequences.

9 Our Natural Tonge is Rude

We can become quite emotional about language matters. We declare some languages or varieties of a language to be beautiful, logical, melodious, or clear, while we decry others as ugly, poor, harsh, or degenerate. For example, glottal stops and "guttural" sounds are sometimes considered to be ugly. How do you test such claims? An Arab is unlikely to be convinced that all those sounds made in the throat in speaking Arabic are ugly. In much of British English the *r* in words like *farm* and *car* remains unpronounced; in much of North America it is pronounced. What claims legitimately follow? And are there truly esthetic differences between the RP (Received Pronunciation) accent associated with a British public-school education and the inner-city Liverpool accent made popular by the Beatles? Would an untutored visitor from Mongolia know which is likely to be more highly regarded at a meeting of the Royal Society and at a rock concert in Liverpool?

Writing at the beginning of the sixteenth century in *The Boke of Phyllyp Sparowe*, the poet and satirist John Skelton said of English that: "Our natural tonge is rude." But, objectively, what is a "rude tonge" like? How does it differ from one that is not "rude"? On the other hand, Thomas Blount in 1656 praised "our refined English Tongue" and two years later Edward Phillips complimented the language "for elegance, for fluency, and happiness of expression." John Kersey in 1708 admired its "Copiousness, Elegancy, variety of Phrases, and other admirable Beauties." Joseph Addison, writing in the *Spectator* in 1711, described what he called the "genius" of the English tongue. He said that he reveled in the pronunciation of words such as *liberty, conspiracy, theatre*, and *orator*, but also deplored *drown'd, walk'd, arriv'd, mayn't*, and *can't* for the way they had "disfigured" and "clogged" the language, apparently because of the clustering of consonants at the end of each word. Addison concluded by commenting that a language reflects the people who use it, citing English, French, Italian, Spanish, and German as examples.

English has not been alone in earning praise. French has been even more highly praised, especially by the French themselves. Remarkably too, they have been extraordinarily successful in persuading others to join them in singing the praises of French! Perhaps the above writers who praised English were doing no more than trying to demonstrate that English was just as worthy of praise as French.

French has long been widely praised for its clarity, beauty, rigor, and logic. The French write book after book on the subject with quite explicit titles: Daniel Mornet's 1929 *Histoire de la clarté française* and Albert Dauzat's 1944 *Le Génie de la langue française* are just two of the better known examples. A quick glance at almost any book about the French language written by a speaker of French will likely provide further evidence. In one of his letters Diderot has this to say on the subject of the French language: *"Le français est fait pour instruire, éclairer et convaincre; le grec, le latin, l'italien, l'anglais, pour persuader, émouvoir et tromper"* (French is made to instruct, enlighten and convince; Greek, Latin, Italian, English, to persuade, move, and deceive). French opinions to the contrary are rarely voiced; only occasionally will a speaker of French admit that we should not be surprised that French seems to be the clearest of all languages to the French, for, after all, they have been using French all their lives and know it better than they know any other language. We should be surprised only if it were otherwise.

Some French writers have gone further in their claims. Language may mirror thought and some languages may mirror it better than others. Some of the *philosophes* were prepared to argue that French was a better mirror of thought than any other language, Latin being the only possible rival. According to Antoine Rivarol in his *De l'universalité de la langue française* of 1784, the syntax of French best reflected human thought. He added for good measure: *"Ce qui n'est pas clair n'est pas français"* (What is not clear is not French).

Why is French so clear? According to Mornet's book, it is because of the climate of France; according to Dauzat's, it is because of the characteristics of the French "race," that particular combination of the Celtic, Latin, and Germanic people. Rivarol, however, attributed it to the temperament of the people. None of these accounts has any validity.

A "climate" explanation for language differences and characteristics is not unusual. In the nineteenth century the "nasality" and "drawling" of Americans were ascribed to the climate of North America. Climate has also been held to be responsible for differences in culture and social organization, resulting in people being lazy here but hard-working there, or fiercely competitive in one area of the world but very cooperative in another. Unfortunately for this theory, the "exceptions" usually turn out to be at least as numerous as the "rule" in such cases! The theory that climate causes languages to vary in harshness, softness, melodiousness, slowness, quickness, precision, and taciturnity is also false. If a Texas farmer typically "drawls" and a New Yorker seems always to be in a hurry in speaking, what conclusion can we reasonably come to about any other aspect of the language of the two, or about the general relationship of language to climate, culture, thought, and intelligence?

People do come to such conclusions. The Emperor Charles V said that Italian was a language suitable for talk with one's mistress, French for talk with one's fellow men, German for ordering horses about, but Spanish was the language in which to communicate with one's Maker. We can see such attitudes in the modern world too. Bengalis living in Assam in India do not like to have to use Assamese in their work because they regard Assamese as a language that is much inferior to Bengali. In at least one dispute Bengalis carried posters declaring Assamese to be a donkey's language – only to be countered with Assamese posters declaring Bengali to be a goat's language!

In an Appendix to *Dissertations on the English Language* Noah Webster quotes a letter from Benjamin Franklin to a certain Miss S. In that letter Franklin criticizes the view that Spanish is finely pronounced, Italian is effeminate, and English is harsh. He points out that this view is based on vague ideas that Spaniards are chivalrous, Italians have some inclination toward opera, and English contains certain words that are crowded with consonants and uses lots of monosyllabic words. He calls such ideas about differences "random and fantastic," and he is right. But Franklin undermines his own arguments when he goes on to say that "rude or uncultivated" peoples, specifically citing "mountaineers," "hunters," and "peasants," must have languages that are restricted and lacking in "general poetic power." He cites the examples of Gaelic, Hebrew, Welsh, Manx, and Armoric, although he concedes that some who used them may have been "occasionally gifted."

In Franklin's view a language needs "cities and the habits of luxurious people" to flourish. He admits that a language may offer its speakers an advantage because it has certain grammatical features. He points out that the two-gender system of French limits that language in comparison with English, because the availability of a "neuter" in English provides a "means of creating light, and a more potent vitality." All we can safely conclude from these various comments is that Franklin preferred English to French and other languages.

10 The Genius of a Language

The idea that there is a close, possibly determining, relationship between a language and the people who speak it is widespread. In this view a language expresses the character of the people who use it. This idea can be found in writers such as Herder, Joseph Addison, Johann Gottlieb Fichte, Wilhelm von Humboldt, and Karl Vossler. In an essay in the *Spectator* in 1711 Addison declared: "I have only considered our Language as it shows the Genius and natural Temper of the *English*, which is modest, thoughtful and sincere." In his *Address to the German Nation* of 1807 Fichte praised the German language and allied it to national aspirations. He declared that German had a natural superiority over all other languages, a superiority that could be extended to those who spoke it. Von Humboldt maintained that the spirit of a people shone through its language. Rousseau had said much the same in *Émile* when he declared that *"l'esprit en chaque langue a sa forme particulière"* (each language has its particular spirit). Otto Jespersen, writing in *Growth and Structure of the English Language*, found the English language "positively and expressly *masculine*, it is the language of a grown-up man and has very little childish or feminine about it," a remark that is clearly "sexist" by today's standards.

According to Vossler in *The Spirit of Language in Civilization* of 1932, each language has "something akin to a soul and an individuality" or its own "psychic aspect," which points its speakers in certain directions. Language both fashions a people and becomes the people. According to Vossler, the French "national character is embodied and realized in what we call the French language." He adds: "The French language, therefore, is the *whole* of the French mind." Furthermore, "the genius or language spirit of a nation is no mythological being; it is a force, a talent, a temperament." Speaking of German, Vossler finds in Goethe's poems a "Germanness . . . due not so much to the use of language according to accepted rules, as to the actual concrete and spiritual nature of the German language."

Such beliefs can be dangerous, but they are widely held. Rarely does a group willingly give up its language to adopt the language of another group. Language is like ethnicity, religion, and territory. It is something that many are willing to fight for and, if necessary, die for. They do this because of a belief in the essential appropriateness to them of a particular language. It is easy to see how such a belief can be extended to regard a particular language as being "better" than all others.

Wars can be fought over language issues or the consequences can be less severe. The inability of Canadians to agree on an appropriate relationship between the English and French languages in Canada has bedeviled Canadian history. British and American English are also slightly different, but are they so different that they should be regarded as separate languages? How valid is the statement in many French translations of Amerian books that they are "translated from the American"? Was H. L. Mencken right to title his 1919 masterpiece *The American Language* and argue that this language was "better" than the variety spoken across the Atlantic? Should Illinois in 1923 have proclaimed the "American language" its official language rather than the English language? Were Americans in the nineteenth century justified in their belief that "many [Americans] speak better than in England"? And what about those speakers of British English who look with disfavor on the varieties of "their" language spoken in North America and "down under" in Australia?

Should we agree with John Adams, the second president of the United States, in a letter to the President of Congress in 1780, that the English language can be associated with the idea of liberty? Adams contrasted this association of English with liberty with the association of other languages with non-democratic beliefs. Earlier, some of the *philosophes* had puzzled over how a great language like French could have become associated with the totalitarian rule of Loius XIV. In the twentieth century, George Orwell made similar remarks concerning German, Russian, and Italian. In this case Orwell was concerned with the "decline" of these languages, which he attributed to "dictatorship." A survey of the relationship between languages and various forms of government might produce some interesting findings at the end of the twentieth century but support for the above claim would not be one of them. Nor is there is any reason to believe that there should be such support.

If there is no such thing as the genius of a language, perhaps we may still be able to maintain that individual human geniuses are largely responsible for certain languages. For example, there is a widespread belief that English owes much of its genius to William Shakespeare (with possibly some small credit also going to Geoffrey Chaucer), to the compilers of the King James Bible of 1611 and The Book of Common Prayer, and to the dictionary-maker Samuel Johnson. (Winston Churchill is occasionally given a nod too.) In the same vein Dante is given considerable credit for Italian, and Martin Luther and Johann Wolfgang von Goethe for German.

Voltaire expressed his opinion about the importance of such geniuses in a letter to a friend in 1761: *"Si le peuple a formé les langues, les grands hommes les perfectionnent par les grands livres"* (If people have made languages, great men perfect them in great books). That claim might not be true; we should at least consider the possibility that it is not. Great writers must inevitably use the language of the times in which they write. They can and do exploit the resources they find. It is their particular genius to do so. However, they are inevitably limited by the need to make sense to their contemporaries, as Shakespeare well knew, and this requirement severely limits what they can do.

Dante recognized the artificiality of the Italian he had created from the various dialects and knew how important it was to rely most heavily on his native Florentine. What such writers do is give permanent expression to the language of a particular period. They exploit existing practices and, by being extremely good at what they do, highlight these practices for those who follow. That is how they achieve their effect. They produce fine works that live on. So Shakespeare's plays and the words of that Bible continue to influence us today and leave the impression that they have, in a very significant way, shaped the actual language we use. We really must ask ourselves how different the English language we use today would have been if Shakespeare had never lived. It is hard to see what substantive differences there would have been, certainly in its grammar, sounds, and vocabulary. English literature would have been different and our store of idioms would be less full, but those are other issues. The English language would have a different flavor to it but that is all.

11 A Sweet Disorder

People subscribe to a wide variety of beliefs about language and they quite readily give expression to them. Language is such an intimate part of our reality that each of us can set up as an expert on language matters. However, true expertise demands disciplined study of the relevant phenomena and what often passes for expertise in language has little or no basis in any kind of discipline. It is almost entirely the product of a mixture of intuition (which tells us that the sun goes round the earth), speculation (which encourages us to buy lottery tickets rather than to save for the proverbial rainy day), superstition (which eliminates a named thirteenth floor on many office and apartment buildings), and a failed education in language (which among other things tells us that English has exactly eight parts of speech, that *ain't* is not a word, and that *It is I* is "better" that *It's me)*.

Our views of language are disordered and often irrational. There is little or no coherence to them. However, this disorder and irrationality is so pervasive and often so enticing that we should try to understand it. It is part of our culture and is not about to go away. Nor are attempts by those who hold some kind of ordered, rational view, i.e., professional students of language, likely to change matters much. They have not in the past and there is little reason to believe that they will do so in the future.

When we do attempt to seek an ordered, rational view we must also be prepared to use language itself with some sense of scientific precision. In a recent book *The Search for the Perfect Language*, Umberto Eco looks at some of the history of attempts to discover an original language and to create a perfect language. He concludes: "Our mother tongue was not a single language but rather a complex of all languages. Perhaps Adam never received such a gift in full; it was promised to him, yet before his long period of linguistic apprenticeship was through, original sin severed the link. Thus the legacy that he has left to all his sons and daughters is the task of winning for themselves the full and reconciled mastery of the Tower of Babel." Such words fit well with the subject matter that Eco has been discussing for some 350 pages. It is such "problems" that the writers he has discussed had dealt with. However, Eco's own words are entirely metaphorical. They are a grand flourish with which to end a book but are also an obstacle themselves to anyone trying to arrive at testable scientific claims. However, in that respect they are thoroughly representative of much "informed opinion" about language.

Our Untied
Tongues

A frequently made observation about English is that its health is not what it should be. People are not using the language properly; they are abusing it. Standards, whatever these are, are not what they once were. Many who use English are corrupting and debasing it. There is a lack of discipline in how we use words. A self-chosen few believe that they must defend the language or we will find ourselves unable to talk to others as chaos results. Such observations have been made for a long time – and will likely continue to be made into the foreseeable future – but we have still somehow managed to survive. We do talk to others, and there is no reason to assume that we will not be able to do so in the future.

Much of the concern arises from the variety we find in the language. What should we do about it? Should we control it and make everyone use English in the same way? And if so, which way? How should we constrain ourselves – and our tongues? Who should tell us what to do and believe? Or should we tolerate a variety of usages and avoid making unwarranted judgments about those we do not care for, particularly when we do not know exactly why we do not care for them?

A few examples will show something of the problem. Many speakers use *more unique*. Should we try to eliminate it from the language, as Henry Fowler's *A Dictionary of Modern English Usage* of 1926 would have us do because "it is nonsense to call anything *more, most, very, somwhat, rather,* or *comparatively unique*"? In this view things are unique or not, perfect or not; there can be no degrees of uniqueness and perfection. Or should we recognize that vast numbers of people see nothing wrong with evaluating uniqueness and perfection? Does not the constitution of the United States declare: *We the people of the United States, in order to form a more perfect union . . .?*

If, as Sterling Leonard found in his 1932 study *Current English Usage, I feel badly* is in widespread use among educated people, should we tolerate it alongside *I feel bad*? How are we to resolve disputes about which usage is "better"? We could declare one of the two expressions to be "proper English" and proscribe the other, but we should heed the proverb: "Easier said than done." Which one of us when looking at a group photograph that includes oneself would say *Which one is I?* or remark *Oh, that's I*? But there are those who must be tempted to speak that way. And would anyone ever exclaim *God knows whom!*? To make sense of these issues, we must try to appreciate some of the variety that exists in our language and be aware of what has been said about that variety.

1 An Aggravating Lot of Words

If we look closely at the words in our language we find that over time we lose some, add others, and change the meanings of not a few. If only such changes did not occur and – like Gertrude Stein's rose ("A rose is a rose is a rose") – a word stayed a word stayed a word! It might also help if we had a single, authoritative dictionary which has "frozen" the meanings of words for all time – or at least for a long time – and told us which words are "in the language" and, therefore, which ones are not! Then we could be sure whether a particular word exists and, if it does, what it really means and how it should be pronounced, spelled, and so on. However, living languages do not work that way, nor can they be made to do so. A language is what it is, and words are what they are.

Words that have dropped out of the language do not usually concern us; we are generally unaware of them. Only when we read older literature or certain kinds of "historical" novels do we come across them. If we were to look at the Lord's Prayer written in Old English, the version of our language that was current about a thousand years ago, we would find *rice* instead of *kingdom* and *costnunge* instead of *temptation*. Other Old English words like *neata*, *se*, and *frumsceaft* have been replaced respectively by *cattle*, *the*, and *creation*. This is just a small sample of words that have disappeared from our language.

Words that come into the language or that change their meanings, however, are noticeable and occasionally cause concern. Toward the end of the sixteenth century Angel Day, the author of a book on rhetoric entitled *The English Secretarie*, heaped scorn on the need to use words such as *exasperate* and *arcane*, and George Puttenham, the author of *The Art of English Poesie* in 1589, deplored the use of *audacious* and *compatible*. These words are completely inoffensive today.

In 1756 an article in the *Critical Review* expressed disapproval of words like *appendage, propelled, condemnable, tranquillity, emanate, orient, occident, devastated*, and *bilious*. In 1781 the *Gentleman's Magazine* criticized the Bishop of Lichfield for using certain words in his sermons preached at the University of Cambridge, among them *symbolize, emblematize, solemnify*, and *sanction*. Samuel Johnson himself looked with disfavor on *multifarious, transcendental, ramification, exacerbation*, and *inanity*, all "learned" words. Simpler words than these drew his disapproval too: *blackguard, cajole, clutter, fib, funk, fuss, glum, lad, sham, slim, squelch, stingy*, and *width*.

Many other words found disfavor in the eighteenth century: *banter, begot, coax, enthusiasm, extra, flippant, flimsy, frisky, fun, jilt, mob, nervous, quandary, shabby, snob, squabble*, and *touchy*. We must ask ouselves what our language would be like today if we did not have these words. We might wonder what made them so objectionable to those who condemned them at the time.

Such condemnation did not stop in the eighteenth century; it continued into the following century. For example, Noah Webster was criticized for including such words as *demoralize, Americanize, deputize, advisory*, and *presidential* in his dictionaries. In *Words and their Uses* of 1870 and *Every-day English* of 1880 Richard Grant White, a frequent commentator on language for the *New York*

Times and *Galaxy*, condemned the way in which authors such as Chaucer, Milton, and Shakespeare had used certain words. He voiced his disapproval of *donate, initiate, presidential,* and *reliable,* and said that he preferred *irritate* to *aggravate, earth* to *dirt, leader* to *editorial, station* to *depot, iced-cream* to *ice-cream, railway* to *railroad, photographist* to *photographer,* and either *sciencist* or *scientialist* to *scientist.* His pedantry led him to insist that a man could not be married to a woman; the woman must be married to the man because *marry* was derived from *mari* (husband). Again in the nineteenth century, Edward Gould in *Good English; or, Popular Errors in Language* of 1867 roundly condemned *jeopardize, leniency,* and *underhanded,* and insisted that *journal* could be used only to describe a daily publication.

We could continue in the same vein into the twentieth century – and we will undoubtedly be able to continue into the twenty-first. The BBC in its 1981 publication *The Spoken Word,* a guide for announcers, declared against *aggravate* used in the sense of *annoy,* certain uses of words such as *anticipate, decimate, disinterested, flaunt, refute, transpire,* and *imply,* and any relaxation of the prescriptive rule for the use of *lie* and *lay.* It would be easy to add other examples to such a list: *alibi* meaning *excuse,* and words like *concept, commitment, interface, prioritize* (in fact almost any word ending in *-ize* in the view of some critics), and *viable.*

Not only do new words come into the language but many words change their meanings as the world changes. When we read Shakespeare's plays, we must be constantly on the alert to his language. Words like *awful, clergy, character, wench, wit, gentle, bachelor, sad, silly, very,* and *honesty* had different meanings in Shakespeare's time from those they have today.

While we may be able to accept the fact that words like *house, work,* and *sport* cover different ranges of meaning in southern California, Glasgow, and Melbourne, and must have meant something different a century ago from what they mean today, we may be reluctant to accept the full consequences of this idea for language as a whole. Words are not fixed entities with the same values everywhere and for all time. Their values are negotiable and move this way and that like the values of currency on a free-market money exchange. We know what happens when people try to fix the value of a currency in arbitrary fashion; its value becomes artificial so that some day the currency loses its credibility, like the former Soviet Union's ruble at the beginning of the 1990s. The same thing would happen to fixed values given to words; they would become irrelevant and another set of words would replace them in one way or another.

Problems of meaning arise constantly. What do *beer, sausage, brie, feta cheese, sherry, brandy, chocolate,* and *chocolate milk* mean? What substances do they refer to? The 1990s saw much disagreement in Europe on this matter as an attempt was made to standardize product labeling for traded goods. Such trade descriptions are part of modern life but not a part that all welcome since "correct" and "incorrect" naming here has important consequences.

New words come into the language all the time: the compilers of every new dictionary make a point of telling us some of the new words they have included, recently words like *aerobics, Afro, AIDS, bikini, braindrain, childproof, crack, disinformation, disco, frisbee, miniskirt, modem, power lunch, privatize, quasar, sputnik, yuppie,* and *zip code.* We may not like some of these because they are symptomatic of values we do not wish to share, but they are now part of the language. They will continue to stay in the language if they prove to be useful but only for so long as they are useful. Some may also change their meanings.

Words can change their meanings in various ways. Some narrow in their meaning: *meat, deer, cattle, flesh, fee,* and *liquor* all once had much wider meanings than they have today. Robert Louis Stevenson used *meat* where we would use *food* in *A Child's Garden of Verses*:

> It is very nice to think
> The world is full of meat and drink.

Shakespeare is using *deer* with the sense of our modern *animal* when in *King Lear* we find:

> But mice and rats and such small deer
> Have been Tom's food for seven long year.

Some words acquire a little more "glamor" as the years pass, e.g., *earl, lord, lady,* and *steward.* Few people today see a connection between the last of these words and *sty,* as in *pigsty.* On the other hand, other words take on pejorative associations, e.g., *wench, cunning, crafty, villain, stench, hussy, lewd,* and *silly.* A silly person was once one who was blessed!

Other changes occur. *Gay* has shifted its meaning dramatically in the last two decades. The following lines by William Wordsworth must cause some occasional difficulties in interpretation today:

> A poet could not but be gay
> In such a jocund company.

How many recognize the connections between *hysteria* and *hysterectomy, delapidated* and *lapidary,* and *cunning* and *conning* (as in a submarine's *conning tower)* with both words once meaning "learning"? The verb *learn* once included *teach* in its meaning, as it still does for those who say *That'll learn you!*

If words do shift their meanings in such ways, what is so "bad" about using *alibi* in the sense of *excuse* or *aggravate* in the sense of *annoy?* In discussing *decimate* used in the sense of *damage* or *destroy* in *Language is Power,* John Honey asks: "is it still too late to take action . . .?" In his view a useful distinction is being lost. However, distinctions are lost all the time when words shift their meanings (and, conversely, new distinctions arise). People who are concerned with such matters focus their attention on a few words that are changing their meanings in an attempt to stop that change; they ignore other changes that are occurring. Such people are often influential or wish to be considered so. Others who value their opinions must know which words are currently being given such attention if they are not to offend those who profess to care about the language. However, it is doubtful that any lasting effects result from this attention. The change – or "misuse," as it is sometimes called – will almost certainly continue until in some cases it may wipe out the old meaning. In other cases the old and new meanings may last side by side in the language for centuries. This is the only way we can explain a thousand years of "problems" with *lie* and *lay,* and *learn* and *teach.*

2 Hopefully, I'll Get it Right

Hopefully has become one of the most discussed words in English for those who worry about the future of that language; they do see a future but fear it may be one of decline. They strive hopefully to see that this word is used properly so as to prevent further erosion in the language. Should we add: *Hopefully, they may succeed*? Obviously not, if they are to succeed. But why is that last use of *hopefully* "bad" whereas the use of *obviously* in the preceding sentence is "good"?

English has a number of adverbs like *obviously*, e.g., *incidentally, definitely, understandably*, and *confidentially*. We can use them to modify whole sentences as in the above example with *obviously*, in which *if they are to succeed* is modified by *obviously* (plus *not*). So we have sentences like *Incidentally, what do you want for your birthday?*, *Understandably, John was concerned*, and *Certainly, he can go*. Many speakers of English have added *hopefully* to this list.

Some would-be protectors of the language do not think *hopefully* belongs there: for example, William Strunk, Jr and E. B. White in the second edition of *The Elements of Style* of 1972 tell us that: "Such use is not merely wrong, it is silly." They add that: "To say, 'Hopefully I'll leave on the noon plane' is to talk nonsense." But that is exactly what many people do say and it is extremely doubtful that they are ever misunderstood when they say it. Strunk and White add: "Although the word in its new, free-floating capacity may be pleasurable and even useful to many, it offends the ear of many others, who do not like to see words dulled and eroded, particularly when the erosion leads to ambiguity." A sentence adverb is not ambiguous, it does not "free-float" whatever that means, and a word is neither dulled nor eroded when it takes on a new use. Moreover, *Hopefully, he will not do it again* seems as "good" as *It is to be hoped he will not do it again*, particularly to anyone who wants to avoid the directness of *I hope he will not do it again*.

The argument that appeals to potential ambiguity is a very weak one. Not even double negatives such as *He didn't do nothing about it* are ambiguous; only the perverse insist they are. There is no ambiguity in Chaucer's Prologue to *The Canterbury Tales* when he says of the knight:

> He nevere yet no vileyne ne sayde
> In al his lyf unto no maner wight.

When a writer does use two negatives together to "make a positive," it can give a reader serious pause. In *Running in Place*, writing of a goat that had escaped from confinement, Nicholas Delbanco says: "She capered and leaped down the rock wall, evasive, a creature unused to no cage." Not the easiest phrase to comprehend in standard English! In one case an insistence that a word has only one use creates ambiguity. Anyone who insists that *like* must be used only as a preposition and cannot be used as a conjunction must reject *Do it like I do it* in favor of *Do it as I do it*. However, whereas *Do it as I do it* is ambiguous *Do it like I do it* is not.

Numerous other words and expressions receive the *hopefully* treatment from the word-watchers. For example, English has a long history of using words like *slow, deep, loud, tight*, and *easy* as adverbs. These are unmarked – or flat – adverbs with a history going back to Old English. Adverbs ending in -*ly* are a more recent addition to the language. Consequently, sentences like *The moon shone bright and clear in the night sky, Drive slow, Dive deep for it, Don't play it so loud, Hold tight*, and *Take it easy* are perfectly good English sentences and always have been so.

We have words – and they are also adverbs – like *brightly, easily*, and *deeply*. They have their own uses: *Brightly shone the moon that night, It's easily understood*, and *She's deeply troubled*. There is no justification for insisiting that we must give up *Drive slow* for *Drive slowly* or *Dive deep* for *Dive deeply*. What we have are two forms for each adverb; what we do not have is adjectives being used where adverbs are "required." *Slow* and *deep* are both adjectives and adverbs, and have been so for a long time. In such cases we are being asked to abandon an important, old characteristic of the language, the flat, i.e., uninflected, adverb, for a more recent innovation. Those who "care" enough to ask us to do this often do not care enough to make sure their facts are correct. We must remember, however, that it is not facts that are important to them;

it is opinions based on randomly acquired impressions of what is "proper" or "improper."

Momentarily, as in *We will be landing momentarily* or *Please hold and a ticket agent will be with you momentarily*, is another example of a well-watched word. Further examples abound. Which word should follow *different*? *From, to*, or *than*? Should it be *compared to* and *contrasted with* or *compared with* and *contrasted to*? According to John Simon, a frequent commentator on the decline and fall of the English language, writing in *Paradigms Lost*, the first pair is to be preferred to the second pair not for any logical reason – what could be a possible logical reason? – but because they are "correct," although what makes them correct Simon never tells us. Likewise, *come and see* gains the seal of approval but *try and do* or *try and get* do not. And so on and so on and so on.

3 'Enry 'Iggins Meets Eliza Doolittle'

The correct pronunciation of words is another issue that brings expressions of concern. However, correctness varies with who is speaking, where, and for what purpose! It must mean different things for a Houston oil worker, a Bostonian patrician, a Scot from Aberdeen, a surfboarder from Brisbane, and a BBC announcer in London. English would be a less interesting language if its words were everywhere pronounced in the same way. Given the social and geographical distribution of the language, English is unlikely ever to be spoken uniformly nor should we wish it might be so.

Consequently, some upper-class British speakers may pronounce *powerless* as though it were *parlous*, *fire* like *fah*, *man* like *men*, and *hope* like *hape*. They do not pronounce the *r* in words like *farm*, *worm*, and *car*, but most Americans, unless they are from the South, or New England, do pronounce the *r*s in such words. Wheras *r*-dropping in such words is increasing in England it is decreasing in North America. *Ant* and *aunt* will have different vowels in this British variety, and the vowel of *bath*, *pass*, and *last* will be different from that of *ant* and *cat*. There is, therefore, no one, universal way to pronounce *man, pass, farm, aunt*, and *fire* "correctly." A particular pronunciation is "correct" for a particular group of speakers and "incorrect" for others. "Correctness" is a relative concept.

If we listen to the way speakers of English pronounce the language, we can find many interesting variations. There are different regional and social pronunciations and also variations within these. There are different pronunciations for words like *either, amen, data, economics, tomato, nephew, process, ration,* and *leisure.* What is the vowel in *book, blood, root, roof, food, room, soot,* and *tooth*? Is it the same in all these words? May it differ on occasion, as, for example, between *tooth* and *toothbrush*? Why do we have such variation? The answer has to do with the history of the vowel that the *oo* spelling represents. It used to be pronounced like the vowel in *boat.* However, about five centuries ago the vowel shifted in quality to become like that of the vowel in *fool.* Later, that new vowel shifted in certain words to become like the vowel in *good* and sometimes as far as the vowel in *mud.* Different dialects treat the words in the above list according to this progression but have not moved words along it in the same way. In the first chapter I described my own experience with the pronunciation of *book.*

Another kind of variation is in words like *tune* and *duke,* and also *graduate, India, individual, cordial, grandeur,* and *issue.* Some speakers pronounce the *d* s, *t* s, and *s* s in these words as they do in *din, tin,* and *sin;* others are influenced by the following vowel and palatalize the consonants so that *India* sounds like *Inja* (and *Indian* like *Injun*), *cordial* like *corjal, issue* like *ishue,* and so on. People vary in what they do in such words. As a result a word like *picture* may be pronounced like *pictyure, pickchure, pickcher,* or even *pitcher. Tuesday* may be pronounced *Tyuzday, Toozday,* or *Chewzday* (and also with a final *-dy* instead of *-day*). The *Toozday* or *Toozdy* pronunciations are a feature of those varieties of English that reject words beginning with *dyu-, tyoo-,* and *nyoo-* pronunciations in favor of *doo-, too-,* and *noo-* in words like *dune, tune,* and *news.* If speakers try to adopt pronunciations with a *y* for such words when they do not have it as a result of their upbringing, they may find themselves like one announcer for the Canadian Broadcasting Corporation who for years informed listeners that he was about to read the *nyoon nyooz.*

Not everyone agrees which syllable should carry the main accent in words like *explicable, contribute, comparable, primarily, controversy, pejorative, subsidence, mischievous, integral, reputable, clandestine, lamentable, formidable, demonstrable,* and *temporary.* More than one possibility exists, and we are far from the agreement that we have today about where the main accent lies in *character* and *illustrate.* Not so long ago these last two words carried their main accent on the second syllable rather than on the first; for a while there must have been two different stress patterns for each of these words, one of which eventually disappeared.

There is disagreement about the desirability of using "reduced" pronunciations of words and of individual vowels within words. *Can, and,* and *that* (as in *the one that I want*) do not usually have the vowel of *cat, the* does not usually have the vowel of *bed,* and *of* does not usually have the vowel of *Don.* Instead, they have an "indistinct" unstressed vowel, one that linguists call "schwa," the same vowel we find at the beginnings of words like *about, attack,* and *upon,* at the end of *coma,* and in the unstressed final syllables of *little, rabbit,* and *button.* Spoken English requires these "reduced" vowel pronunciations. We are not "slurring" or being lazy when we speak like this; we are behaving naturally as native speakers.

This natural pronunciation of English does have some potential dangers. It may lead some of us to use spellings like *He could of gone* when the accepted way of writing what we say in this case is *He could've gone.* In everyday speech no native speaker of the language says *He could have gone* with *have* containing the vowel of *cat.* When people write *pot o' gold, shop 'n' save,* and *Drinka pinta milk,* they are deliberately capturing the spoken language for certain purposes.

Sometimes objections are voiced to *I like 'em;* we are told to use *I like them* instead. However, *I like 'em* is a very appropriate English utterance. It not only nicely indicates the reduced stress on the final vowel, but also may not even involve a reduction of *them* to *'em.* The Old English third person plural pronoun did not begin with *th-;* it began with *h-.* After the Scandinavian invasions of the ninth century English found itself with two third person plural pronouns, one beginning with *th-* and one without, the one with *th-* having been acquired from the invaders. There is good reason to believe that the pronunciation *I like 'em* is therefore "older" than the *I like them* pronunciation.

One of the reasons why some people get upset about certain pronunciations is that they regard them as diverging too far from the spellings of words. A long-standing belief exists that the spelling of a word should tell us how to pronounce that word. We do accept some spellings as being completely idiosyncratic, burdensome, etymological relics. The English village, also my native parish, named *Ulgham*, pronounced like *Uffam*, is one, and so are other English names like *St John, Cholmondeley, Beauchamp, Daventry, Cirencester, Pepys*, and either *Magdelen* or *Magdelene*, the colleges at Oxford and Cambridge respectively. However, there is a common belief – and not an entirely unreasonable one – that we should be able to use spelling as a guide to pronunciation. In order to do so we would need to decide which pronunciations are "correct." Who gets to make such decisions?

The English spelling system requires us to write many letters we do not pronounce. These include the double-letter convention in words like *running* and *sitting*, the use of certain letter combinations – in this case imported into the language many hundreds of years ago by French-trained scribes – like *sh, ch*, and *th* in words like *shop, cheap*, and *thin* or *then*, and the use of *s* for both the *s* sound at the end of *cats* and the *z* sound at the end of *beds*. We have only to look at any discussion of "spelling reform," i.e., the claimed need for it, to find many more examples of such conventions and "inconsistencies" that proponents claim should be changed or regularized on one or other principle.

The great temptation is to insist that certain letters should be pronounced because they are there in the written language. For example, how should we pronounce *Wednesday* and *February*? As long ago as the fifteenth century, speakers of English had ceased pronouncing the boldfaced letters in the following words: *ki**l**n, **d**amn, conde**m**n, cup**b**oard, rasp**b**erry, han**d**some, han**d**kerchief, Christ**m**as*, and *ches**t**nut*. Today, some people pronounce some of these letters under the influence of spelling. The same loss also occurred in the following words in the places indicated; however, in these words there has been a widespread restoration of the pronunciation of the letter: *to**w**ards, Lon**d**on, hus**b**and, We**d**nesday, stric**t**, of**t**en, respec**t**, mos**t**ly, fa**l**con*, and *so**l**dier*. Other words with pronunciations that are often heavily influenced by their spellings are *forehead,* *again, been, waistcoat, comparable, comely, Coventry,* and *Ralph.* Consequently, each of the above words – and there are others like them – has more than one pronunciation. *Often* pronounced without a *t* may be found alonsgside *often* pronounced with a *t.* The first pronunciation is every bit as legitimate as the second, as legitimaté as the pronunciation of *soften* (no *t* there). Speakers who have no *t* in their pronunciation of *often* are not being lazy and are not dropping the *t;* they are using a pronunciation that has been in the language for hundreds of years, one not influenced by spelling.

Spelling pronunciations can lead users of the language badly astray. *Meet* and *meat* were once pronounced with different vowels, which accounts for the spelling difference we see today. These words were pronounced alike by the fifteenth century, but some teachers of the language tried to insist that the two vowels were different for at least two more centuries. Today, no-one teaching English would make that mistake. However, many teachers insist on teaching children that words beginning with *wh-* (but not *who*), e.g., *which, when,* and *what,* begin with a diffferent sound from words beginning with *w-* alone, e.g., *witch, went,* and *watch.* Nearly every book on phonics insists that this difference exists everywhere in English and is an important one for children who are learning to read to become aware of. However, in most varieties of English this *wh-/w-* distinction has not existed for at least two centuries. For example, John Walker observed in *A Critical Pronouncing Dictionary* of 1791 that Londoners no longer pronounced the *h* in words like *white, where,* and *why.* (He deplored that this was so as he also deplored the loss of *h* in words like *harm* and *heart.*) The language loses almost nothing by our failure to distinguish the pronunciations of *which* and *witch.* Even if we made such a distinction, it would not be important because it would apply to so few words all of which are kept apart in other ways, i.e., they are different parts of speech. Time spent on teaching this distinction is time wasted and may even result in pronunciations like *whoe* (for *woe*) and *Whednesday.*

"Dropping initial *h* s and final *g* s" is the ultimate crime committed by those who do not follow spelling slavishly. Various factors come into play with *h-* dropping. Initial *h* is a very weak consonant and in some varieties of English it disappears without trace. As long ago as 1763, Thomas Sheridan commented in *A Course of Lectures on Elocution* on "the omission of the aspiration in many words by some, and in most by others." He believed that this loss of "one great fund of force and expression" was harmful to the language. However, many speakers of English do say things like *'urry up, 'Enry 'Iggins!* Some go so far as to introduce *h* s where *h* s are not required because they have been told that *h*-prononuncing is prestigious. Those who try to follow the "rules" find that these vary. Words of English origin beginning with *h* usually have that *h* pronounced in the standard variety of the language: *he, heaven, help, heart*, etc. However, words introduced from French show some variety: we do not pronounce the *h* in *honor, hour, honest*, and *heir*, but *herb, hotel, humble*, and *humor* may be found with or without the *h* pronounced. Some say *an hotel* but others say *a hotel*, some *an historical occasion* but others *a historical occasion*, and *Herb* and *herb* may be pronounced differently. It is not surprising that Eliza Doolittle had such a problem with dear old 'Enry 'Iggins in *My Fair Lady*, the musical adaptation of Shaw's *Pygmalion*.

The *-ing* endings on verbs are also viewed as problematic. Any serious student of the history of the English language knows that *-in* has always existed alongside *-ing* as a verbal ending and that *-in* is not a reduced form of *-ing*, i.e., it is not historically *-in'* at all. We know that from the seventeenth century on many people decided that *-ing* should replace *-in*. This replacement is still not complete. As late as the 1920s and 1930s many older, well-to-do speakers of English in England went *huntin, shootin, 'n' fishin*. (You had to be well-to-do in order to do that in England!) Today, such pronunciations tend to be looked down on, but almost everyone uses them on some occasion or other. They occur frequently in relaxed, informal speech as we might expect, if for no other reason than that is the kind of speech least influenced by conscious awareness of spelling and which best preserves the historical continuity of the spoken language. (We should note that this so-called *g*-dropping never occurs in word stems like like *sing* and *hang* but only in participles like *singing* and *hanging*.)

Each major radio and television networks has a stylebook that tells announcers how they must try to pronounce certain words. In 1982 the BBC, for example, in *The Spoken Word*, issued instructions about the way in which it wanted its announcers to pronounce words such as *comparable, deity, kilometre, research*, and *temporarily.* What announcers actually do is another matter, and most of us from time to time hear pronunciations over the airwaves that strike us as being different from those we might have expected. A common reaction in such circumstances is to go to a dictionary for "the truth." However, if we consult a good dictionary we inevitably find that the truth we seek has many faces. A good dictionary will show us some of the variety that exists in pronunciations. One criticicm of *Webster's Third* was that it contained too many alternative pronunciations for certain words. Some critics had wanted the dictionary to approve a single pronunciation for each word and, by not reporting others, indicate in that way its approval and disapproval. They protested loudly when the dictionary did not accept this role.

4 Laziness, Shiftlessness, or Ignorance

The language around us is not uniform, never has been, and never will be. That is the nature of language. But that it is not uniform has long been a source of complaint. The chosen reemedy is to prescribe usage.

In ancient Rome the rhetorician Quintilian observed in *Institutio oratoria* that Latin was spoken well by comparatively few people. We must remember that the Latin that has come down to us is the Latin of the written language of the time. Most people spoke vulgar Latin, the Latin of the people, and it is from this variety that the modern Romance languages developed. They did not develop from the classical written Latin with which we may be familiar. Medieval Latin is another variety of Latin with which certain scholars are familiar.

William Caxton, who introduced printing to England in 1476, had inconsistent views about the English of his time. He could refer to it as "this rude and symple englyssh," but at the same time praise Chaucer for "making [English] ornate and fayr. which shal endure perpetuellye." This was because "hys labour embellyshed/ornated/and made faire our englisshe in thys Royame was had rude speche." (We can note that our first printer was less concerned about spelling than we are today nor did he have a stylebook to follow in matters of usage and punctuation.)

In the sixteenth century English was assailed for its barbarity, baseness, rudeness, and lack of both polish and eloquence. Later, in the eighteenth century, Thomas Sheridan thought that the spoken language was defective and that people did not take enough care when they used it. He was particularly concerned with imprecision in the use of words. Sheridan blamed poor instruction and lack of care among writers for this deficiency. People distrusted the language in Sheridan's day; it seemed to lack the order that much of the social and intellectual leadership of the time craved.

Many of the same criticisms persist today and critics go so far as to bring even the "great" writers to account. Charles Dickens has been criticized for using *like* as a conjunction in *Nobody will miss her like I shall*; Jane Austen for using *different to*; Charlotte Brontë for using *very unique*; and Thomas Hardy for *Who are you speaking of?* In the twentieth century Winston Churchill was criticized for saying: *Hello, America, this is me* in a radio broadcast in 1946.

The French voice similar concerns about their language. In 1746, Voltaire in *Commentaires sur Corneille* criticized Corneille for using *dedans* as a preposition in *Horace*, a tragedy written in 1640. To Voltaire *dedans* had always been and would always be an adverb and Corneille was in error. There is much fertile ground for those who do not like variety in language, particularly any variety other than their own, and who are prepared to use any argument that seems suitable to justify their point of view. When there is no possible argument, a critic can resort to assertion alone.

One such critic is John Simon, a self-declared elitist in his views of language. He describes himself as a precocious, multilingual child who came to England in early adolescence. He now regards himself as a protector of the language he learned there. He makes the self-serving statement that it is people like himself, Joseph Conrad, Karen Blixen, and Vladimir Nabokov, who are not native speakers of the language but who write in it, who have a special advantage that gives them the authority to castigate the natives – or at least gives him that authority.

Simon finds English inconsistent because, as he informs us in *Paradigms Lost*, it arose from an "initial chaos," a claim which he does not substantiate and which could not possibly be true, as anyone who is familiar with the history of English or of any language knows. Simon looks at English and tells us what he likes and dislikes about how people use the language without ever trying to consider why people use it in the various ways they do. Simon and others like him deplore variation because it provides ample evidence of ignorance and bad faith. Like Wilson Follett, one of the staunchest defenders of "standards" in English, Simon ascribes any usages that he himself does not use to "laziness, shiftlessness, or ignorance," Follett's words in a 1960 *Atlantic Monthly* essay entitled "Grammar is Obsolete," a view that tells us much more about the author than it does about the language or any of its uses.

John Honey expresses a less extreme but still unrealistic view of linguistic prescription in *Language is Power*: "the function of prescription is not the prevention of change, but rather the *management* of change – a process of control which allows change to be seen as an orderly process." In this view change is inevitable but should be controlled through prescription. There are, however, serious problems with such an approach. To "manage" a language like this, we would need to know exactly what it is like at any particular time, how language change occurs, and what changes are actually occurring, all topics dear to the hearts of linguists and all difficult ones to research. We would also have to know how to manage change, and no one knows how to do that. We do know that some people try to tinker with bits and pieces of the language but that is another matter and hardly relevant. We do know a lot about managing people and that is what so many self-appointed managers of language are trying to do: manage people not the language.

We see a classic conflict here. There are those who wish to refine and protect the language, who want to uphold the forces of intellect and reason, and who seek for order, clarity, purity, and truth in expression. Against them, they fear, are arrayed the defenders of common or vulgar speeech, those who will allow anything to happen to language, and who seek only to expresss their base passions. A caricature perhaps but like all such portraits not without some truth.

5 The Judge, and Law, and Rule of Speech

Trying to prevent change and impose uniformity is more than a Herculean task, it is an impossible one, much like King Canute's legendary attempt to roll back the tides. Fortunately, there are those who have known this for thousands of years. In Ancient Rome for example, Horace believed that people should become aware of how they use their language and declared that use was the sole arbiter in matters of language and language norms should be derived solely from descriptions of language use. In *De arte poetica* he wrote: *"Quem usus penes arbitrium est et jus et norma loquendi"* (Use is the judge, and law, and rule of speech). Quintilian expressed similar views: *"Sermo constat ratione, vetustate, auctoritate, consuetidine"* (Language is based on reason, antiquity, authority, and use). He added that if there was any conflict among these, the surest guide was use. Later, others like Montaigne, the French essayist of the sixteenth century, echoed this view declaring that, in matters of language, people should prefer custom to arbitrary rule. However, while this is a longstanding view, it is not the most influential.

Language change is both normal and constant, and the relationship of the spoken language to the written language is a complex one. Historically, the written language is derived from the spoken language. Usage in a language may vary considerably and any views concerning "correctness" must be based on a clear understanding of usage and what it means to be "correct." Some people are concerned about such issues and express strong opinions about what should be done. These, too, are facts about the language.

These issues are viewed more urgently in some parts of the English-speaking world than they are in others. North America has the image of being free, relaxed, and informal in many areas of life, but it is British users of English who are more likely to use the language freely and easily, particularly in writing, than North American users. English usage in North America is much more under the influence of those who have been called the "language police," the purists among us.

I will have more to say about such people but let me close this chapter by providing one more piece of evidence as to their reach. The "split infinitive" is a perennial topic: use *to go boldly* not *to boldly go* if we wish to observe the "rule." Here is what *The right Word at the Right Time*, a Reader's Digest publication, says about the split infinitive: "Bear in mind that purists do still object to the split infinitive. If you refuse to pander to this irrational objection of theirs, and if you are unconcerned that people might think you know no better, then by all means split your infinitives. But re-member the possible consequences: your reader or listener may give less credit to your arguments (because he thinks of you as a careless speaker or writer), or he may simply lose the thread of your argument entirely (because he has been distracted by your grammatical 'error')." In other words we should know that while all words and uses of words were created equal they have not stayed that way. Inequality and irrationality are facts of both hu-man and linguistic existence.

CHAPTER FOUR

Words
in Order

We discuss standard English, hear that standards of language use are declining, and are constantly reminded to consult this or that standard reference if we want our language behavior to meet the approval of those who claim to know what standards are. But exactly what are they? Who set them? And why should we be obedient?

There is no standard in English like the standard for the metre, and there is nothing approaching the standard of the length of a particular year or the kind of year we find in the calendar we use. The standard metre has gradually evolved. In its penultimate form it was the length of a bar of platinum kept with great care in a suburb of Paris. Since 1983, however, it is measured by how far a beam of light travels in a certain time in a vacuum. Today, it is the second not the year that is the basic unit of scientifically-kept time, and the atomic clocks that we use to measure years periodically have an extra "leap second" added to them to compensate for the gradual slowing down of the earth's rotation.

The calendar we use every day is not very sophisticated, but it does not have to be. It, too, has had its problems and is a fairly recent innovation. The old Julian calendar inherited from Roman times became badly out of phase with the natural year and had to be replaced by the Gregorian calendar devised in 1582. The calendar change occurred in Britain in 1752, required a shift of more than a week, and led to riots by those who feared their lives were actually being shortened, loss of wages, or even a papist plot. (A modern example of a similar misunderstanding has to do with

Daylight Saving Time and the belief some have that it increases the amount of sunshine that falls on the earth!) The Russians did not make the same calendar change until much later, which is why the anniversary of the October Revolution of 1917 is celebrated on November 7 and Russian Christmas is in early January.

Language does not have standards like these. The word *standard* used in conjunction with *language* as in *standard language* seems to have been used for the first time in print as recently as 1858 in connection with Richard Chenevix Trench's proposal to the Philological Society that led eventually to the publication of the *Oxford English Dictionary*. While the concept of a "standard language" is a recent one, the actual process of standardization in English is a much longer one.

1 Defending and Illustrating a Language

Before turning our attention to developments that resulted in the creation of standard English, we should look at what happened to some other European languages. A standard variety of Latin has existed for two thousand years. This standard derives from the prose of writers such as Cicero and Virgil. Spoken Latin, i.e., vulgar Latin, flourished alongside this classical written language but became, over a period of many hundreds of years, French, Spanish, Italian, and so on, i.e., separate languages in different places. There was also a considerable revival of Latin itself in Europe after the eleventh century as Latin became the language of religion, learning, and the new universities. It was a very different Latin, medieval Latin, and it, too, has left us a considerable body of prose and some verse.

Concurrent with this flowering of medieval Latin there was the growth of the different Romance vernaculars, such as French, Spanish, Italian, and Provençal, but these had none of the prestige of classical Latin nor the uses of medieval Latin. They were the languages of everyday life in the places where they were spoken. They were the languages through which the peoples of particular areas expressed their identities, i.e., the French language

expressed French identity. There was also some vernacular literature. For example, a considerable amount of poetry was written
in Provençal in the twelfth and thirteenth centuries and later in
French itself. However, the people of the time did not think that
these vernacular languages counted for much. They lacked what
written, classical Latin had: an important body of literature and
clearly formulated accounts of how the language appeared to work,
e.g., grammars, lists of accepted spellings, and glossaries.

Those who concerned themselves with the vernaculars believed
that improvements were necessary if these were to achieve the
status of Latin. A language like French would be improved if it
were treated as though it were Latin. It could be brought to order,
given a grammar and a dictionary, and used to develop a body of
literature. Such resources, together with a fixed writing system,
would give it permanence. Some body or bodies would have to
take on the task of defining – or "ascertaining," as the task came
to be called – the new language.

The printing press had been developed by this time. The written forms of language had become readily accesssible to large
numbers of people, and by the sixteenth century much of this
writing was in the vernaculars. There was also a growth of national feeling so that language could readily be associated in people's minds with a higher purpose. Much of the language of religion
might be in Latin, but the language of feeling about being French
or about being English was either French or English. (The French
may not have been as successful in this respect as the English
because it is apparent that even well into the twentieth century
the French were still, as one perceptive commentator on the
French scene has described it, "turning peasants into Frenchmen.")

Those who concerned themselves with trying to provide a foundation for French were initially confused about the origins of the
French language. Some believed that it was Gaulish, i.e., Celtic,
in origin. (The French talk about their Gaulish ancestors.) At the
time when people were trying to give the language some of the
aura associated with Latin, many who tried to do so had little or
no understanding of how the language had evolved. They tended
to attribute to it a linguistically corrupt past in which Celtic, Latin,
and Germanic were haphazardly commingled. This idea lasted

well into the eighteenth century. Today, we know that French is a Romance language derived by well-understood processes from the vulgar Latin spoken in a particular part of the former Roman Empire.

The view persisted that French was not very good and that it should be judged against standards derived from Latin and Greek. There was little respect for medieval French or for the literature of medieval times in general, and it was widely believed that the best literature of that period had been written in Latin. However, some writers were not so pessimistic. In 1549 Joachim du Bellay, a French poet, published *Déffence et illustration de la langue françoyse*. This book drew heavily on – today we would say *plagiarized* – an earlier 1542 work *Diologo delle lingue* by Sperone Speroni on Italian in which Speroni glorified Italian. Du Bellay tried to show the possibilities inherent in French. He admitted that the language had some weaknesses but thought that with a little effort it could be altered, developed, and improved. He also thought that French was a better language than its contemporaries because people he regarded as cultivated were using it, a completely circular observation. He was a man of his time, the Renaissance, in which people thought they could improve the world, in contrast to medieval times, when people tended to look back to the past, to vanished golden ages, and to regret the present moment. Du Bellay's book was not a manual on how to bring glory to French; it was a plea that this could and should be done.

One consequence of this concern for the French language was the founding by Cardinal Richelieu of the Académie Française in 1635 with its mission of bringing order to the language. The academicians were essentially conservative, authoritative, and bourgeois in their beliefs and admirers of literature. The academy published its first dictionary reflecting such views and tastes in 1694, but its first grammar, which was not at all successful, did not appear until 1932. A similar academy had been founded in Italy in 1582, the Accademia della Crusca in Florence, and others followed, e.g., in Spain in 1713.

Just how the French would defend and illustrate their language became a matter of concern. Whose language would they defend and what would they use for illustrations? Claude Favre Vaugelas in his 1647 treatise *Remarques sur la langue françoise* advocated usage not reason as determining what was correct in language. He recommended the usage of *"la plus saine partie de la Cour"* (the healthiest part of the court) which itself would be in accordance with the usage of *"la plus saine partie des Autheurs de ce temps"* (the healthiest part of contemporary authors). However, he acknowledged some drawbacks:*"L'usage fait beaucoup de choses par raison, beaucoup sans raison, et beaucoup contre raison"* (Usage does many things on account of reason, many without reason, and many against reason). For Vaugelas reason alone was not a secure guide in matters of language but when usage and reason fell together that offered the best guarantee.

In this period of the Enlightenment reason seemed to provide the best guide to behavior. A disordered world could be brought to order by the application of pure reason. What was reasonable and logical was to be preferred, in language as in everything else. What was reasonable and logical was also universal. For the *philosophes* of the Enlightenment French was a language of reason. It had a literature, was used in a cultivated society, and was associated with a very important people. It was, however, still imperfect but imperfection could be remedied. Those who were reasonable, educated, literate, and influential could and should decide what was French and what was not.

Consequently, the issue of dealing with perceived imperfections dominated linguistic thought in eighteenth century France. Should you remove these imperfections? Might they not be reasonable in some way? Did chance play any role in languages? How should differences in usage be treated? Who used the language best? There were wide differences of opinion concerning the answers to questions such as these. Voltaire, for example, recognized that French did have some imperfections but was prepared to live with them. However, he did approve of attempts to fix the language for all time in the state that he found it because he thought that any change must be for the worse. On the other hand, the Encyclopedist Diderot wanted to go further; he wanted improvements.

In 1782 Antoine Rivarol, a writer and journalist, in a prize essay entitled *Discours sur l'universalité de la langue française* written for the Berlin Academy at a time when French had great prestige in Europe, declared that French deserved its high esteem because in its subject–verb–object word order it followed the natural and logical order of the world. Moreover, what was not clear was not French. He could not help but contrast French with English, which he saw as having none of the qualities that French had for being a language of science, philosophy, and literature. According to Rivarol, the qualities of French were such that the language should have a universal appeal.

The French continue to pay deliberate attention to their language. The Académie Française makes periodic announcements about language and produces its dictionaries. It is concerned with seeing that French is spoken and written in a certain way and that only certain words are admitted to the language, a not very successful piece of policing if one is familiar with the everyday language of French people who are *au courant* with the world, particularly with the English-speaking world. (Language academies may try to safeguard the literary norm of the language; however, they are virtually powerless when they try to regulate the spoken language.) There are also journals like *Vie et langage*, governmental decrees on the language, and various official groups appointed to look into different matters to do with the language, e.g., large ones like scientific terminology or small ones like the circumflex accent. There are ultimate authorities one can appeal to – but not necessarily follow. Although millions of people who live in France do not think the approved variety of French serves their particular interests, it is, however, the only variety approved for use in government, the law, and education, and is France's only official language of record.

2 Fixing the English Language

English slowly emerged as a national language in the form we know today. There is a noticeable gap between the Old English of a thousand years ago and the Middle English of Chaucer's *Canterbury Tales* and John Wycliife's Bible. Whereas Old English is like a foreign language to us today, neither Chaucer's nor Wycliffe's prose has the same exotic look. Neither used a standard English as we understand that term; each wrote in a variety of English he knew best, preferring that variety to others that existed concurrently. Those choices would ultimately influence which variety of English would come to be promoted as the standard.

The Chancery clerks in Westminster between the years 1420 and 1460 were influential. It was their duty to write the documents the crown required in order to administer the English kingdom. The language they used was English, and a small group of clerks developed a uniform, written language for their work and set a strong example to others. The spread of printing at the end of the fifteenth century, with Caxton and the press he established in Westminster in 1476 the best known event in this development, also tended to reinforce one variety of the language over another. This trend toward uniformity began slowly and in the early days of printing there was no more consistency in the products than there was in the old manuscripts.

The sixteenth century was an exuberant period so far as English was concerned. It was the century of the inventive Shakespeare and of others who wanted to play with the language in various ways. Sir Thomas Elyot, the great neologizer, deliberately set out to improve and promote English by introducing new words into the language. In *The Boke Named the Governour* of 1531, dedicated to Henry VIII and containing a plan for bringing up gentlemen's sons as leaders, Elyot used words borrowed from Latin like "publike and commune" because of "the insufficiencie of our owne langage." However, neologizing could be carried to extremes and the process led to the creation of many "inkhorn" terms, which were added, for the most part temporarily, to the language. This exuberance also led to imitations of classical styles, to the euphuistic ornamentation of prose, to a liking for archaisms, and to excessive repetition.

Characteristic too of the sixteenth century were the mixed views that people had of the language. John Skelton declared that: "Our natural tongue is rude," and Roger Ascham said in *The Scholemaster*, a treatise on education published posthumously in 1570, that English was inadequate as a language in comparison with Latin. In *Toxophilus*, an earlier book on archery, Ascham had said in its dedication that "for the Latin or greke tonge, every thyng is so excellently done in them, than none can do better: In the Englysh tonge contrary, every thinge is in a manner so meanly, bothe for the matter and handelynge than no man do worse." Even though to many at this time English did not appear to be at all "eloquent," Shakespeare was to change that view for many. For example, Richard Mulcaster declared in *The First Part of the Elementarie* of 1582 that: "I love Rome, but London better, I favor Italie, but England more, I honor the Latin, but I worship the English."

Elizabethans thought that English spelling was thoroughly confused. They were concerned that the language lacked sources of authority because there were no dictionaries, grammars, or writings in the language about the language. In 1589 George Puttenham, an English courtier, declared in *The Arte of English Poesie* that poets should model their language on that "of the better brought up sort," for example, the language "spoken in the kings Court." He disfavored the varieties of English spoken in outlying areas such as the borders and sea ports because they would be mixed with other languages. Nor did he think much of the variety of the language associated with the university towns of Oxford and Cambridge: it was too heavily influenced by Latin for his taste. He discounted the varieties of rural areas, those of the lower classes, and those of people living north of the Trent. Puttenham looked to his contemporaries for what he sought, rejecting "the old poets," whose language he said "is now out of use with us." A standard did emerge, but only in post-Elizabethan times. It was based on the variety of English that came to have strong associations with the educated and cultured people who governed England and it found its expression in the King James Bible, which, by the time it was published in 1611, was essentially a conservative document.

The seventeenth century saw little movement toward resolving some of the problems perceived to exist within the language, but English had clearly triumphed over both Latin and French for almost every use. The century saw the development of a considerable literature but without any fixed ideas about what kind of language was appropriate to that literature. The seventeenth century also witnessed considerable political disruption. At its end people once again began to wonder how they might bring order to the language after the restoration of political order. It was clear to those who thought seriously about such matters that English lacked at least two essential appurtenances of a standard language: a dictionary and a grammar. These would lend authority to the language.

A dictionary seems always to have been thought more necessary for a language like French or English than a grammar. After all, to produce a grammar for a language all one had to do was tailor the cloth of a particular vernacular to the Latin pattern that already existed. That was the prevailing view and one not much changed today. Such a possibility does not exist with a dictionary. A dictionary was therefore required if the language were to be "ascertained," or " fixed."

The first English dictionaries were either bilingual dictionaries or glossaries of "hard words." John Palsgrave, a tutor in French in London, published *Lesclaircissement de la langue françoyse* in 1530, an English–French dictionary designed to help people learn French. William Salesbury's *A Dictionary in Englyshe and Welshe* of 1547 was designed to help in the task of teaching English to the Welsh. As an aid, it contained "a little treatyse of the englyshe pronunciation of the letters" of Welsh. There are also many publications in the "hard-words" tradition, i.e., explanations of the meanings of unusual or difficult words. One of the most important was Robert Cawdrey's *A Table Alphabeticall, conteyning and teaching the true writing and understanding of hard usuall wordes, borrowed from the Hebrew, Greeke, Latine, or French* of 1604. It is out of this tradition that our modern dictionary developed, with the major transforming step along the way being Samuel Johnson's dictionary.

Johnson worked in an era in which people were both proud and unsure of the language. For example, the intellectual elite of the eighteenth century held Swift, Addison, and Steele in high regard and admired Shakespeare, Chaucer, and a host of others before these. There was a widespread feeling that English had achieved a kind of golden age during the reign of Queen Anne and that if the language were not quite perfect then it could easily be made so.

Writing in English had become a respectable and profitable profession and writers wanted their work to last. John Dryden, for example, feared that a changing language would mean that his writings would eventually become as difficult to read as Chaucer's were to Spenser and Spenser's were to Dryden's contemporaries. Alexander Pope expressed a similar opinion a little later:

> Our sons their fathers' failing language see,
> And such as Chaucer is shall Dryden be.

Change should be arrested and the language fixed for all time.

In 1712 in a letter to the Earl of Oxford, Jonathan Swift proposed setting up a society for correcting, enlarging, and ascertaining the language "for ever." Swift thought English was "extremely imperfect" and "less refined" than Italian, Spanish, and French, that "in many instances it offends against every Part of Grammar," that any further change would be decline, and that such change could and should be arrested. He expressed his disapproval of the language of the current royal court – in his view its language was corrupt – nor would he look for help to "illiterate Court-fops, half-witted-Poets, and University-Boys," preferring the language of women to those. While Swift's objective was to make the language as good as possible, he did say: "I am of Opinion, that it is better a Language should not be wholly perfect, than that it should be perpetually changing."

While no action was taken on Swift's proposal, Johnson's dictionary did emerge from this climate of concern. In his *Plan of a Dictionary of the English Language* of 1747 Johnson expressed his hope of being able "to fix the English language." He wanted "a dictionary by which the pronunciation of our language may be fixed, and its attainment facilitated; by which its purity may be preserved, its use ascertained, and its duration lengthened." Johnson's own definition of *ascertain* in the dictionary that resulted is: "To make certain; to fix; to establish." Later, in the Preface to his dictionary he admitted to failure because of "the boundless chaos of a living speech." Although Johnson began with the idea that he would be able to fix the language as his contemporaries hoped, the work involved in making the dictionary showed him that he could not fix the language because it kept on changing no matter what anyone did or wanted to do. Johnson quickly learned the lesson that all dictionary-makers learn sooner or later, that a dictionary is out of date on the day of its publication. He learned another lesson too, that making a dictionary involves both "science" and "art," both knowledge of facts and the wisdom to know the best use to make of these facts.

In the Preface to *A Dictionary of the English Language* of 1755, Johnson noted that a dictionary-maker could not "embalm his language, and secure it from corruption and decay." There is a note of failure in that word *decay*, of acknowledgment that the golden age of the language lay in its past. It is a note that other commentators on the language will sound constantly over the next two centuries: the best is somehow behind them and all they can do is raise a valiant defence. Johnson's work made him aware of change; others like Joseph Priestley were aware of change too, and of their powerlessness to legislate against it. Priestley, writer, scientist, and co-discoverer with Lavoisier of oxygen, declared in *Rudiments of English Grammar* of 1761 that "the best forms of speech will, in time, establish themselves by their own superior excellence; and, in all controversies, it is better to wait the decisions of Time, which are slow and sure, than to take those of Synods, which are often hasty and injudicious."

Although Johnson drew considerably on the work of his predecessors, particularly that of Nathaniel Bailey in *An Universal Etymological English Dictionary* of 1721, his dictionary set entirely new standards for dictionary making. Johnson defined *dictionary* as: "A book containing the words of any language in alphabetical order, with explanations of their meaning; a lexicon; a vocabulary; a word-book." For the first time simple words were defined in a dictionary; as he had said in his *Plan*, a proper dictionary should define "*horse, dog, cat, willow, alder, daisy, rose*, and a thousand others." No longer were dictionaries to confine themselves to defining only "hard words."

Johnson's sources were wide and varied, but he drew mainly for his examples on what he called "the wells of English undefiled," great writers like Hooker, Bacon, Raleigh, Spenser, Sidney, and Shakespeare, and from the King James Bible. However, he was a man of his time and his reporting was not free of judgments about what he was reporting on. In discussing words included in the dictionary, he freely used terms such as *barbarous, cant, corrupt* or *corruption, erroneous, false, improper, inelegant, low, ludicrous, mistaken, vitious* (sic), and *vulgar*. Johnson used these terms variously for words like *fuss, cajole, belabour, gambler, simpleton, touchy*, and *volunteer*. In his dictionary Johnson is clearly a self-appointed legislator in matters of language taste. He chooses his sources, for example literary rather than popular ones, and he passes judgment on what he finds. Others are expected to heed his words and accept his judgments.

However, Johnson was not without a sense of humor. How else can we explain his definition of *oats*: "A grain, which in England is generally given to horses, but in Scotland supports the people"? A *lexicographer* is "a harmless drudge" and *Whig* is a "faction." Johnson erroneously defined *pastern* as "the knee of a horse" and, according to his biographer James Boswell, when a woman of his acquaintance asked him why he had done so, he replied "Ignorance, madam, pure ignorance."

Johnson's dictionary, though not initially a commercial success, being quite expensive, was widely applauded. In a letter to the *World* in 1754, Lord Chesterfield, for example, praised Johnson's work of "fixing the language" and said that he would willingly acknowledge Johnson as a "dictator" in lexicographic matters. He associated Johnson's work with "good order and authority." So successful eventually was the dictionary, particularly in an abridged version, that establishing an academy for the English language was no longer deemed to be necessary. Johnson's *Dictionary* supplied English with the authority it needed. Henceforth, dictionaries would always speak with authority.

From time to time moves would still be made to found an academy for English. In the United States John Adams, a future president, in a letter to Congress in 1780, proposed setting up an academy "for refining, correcting, improving, and ascertaining the English language." In this case it was the American variety of the language, but nothing came of Adams' proposal. Other attempts followed, including those by the American Academy of Arts and Letters in 1916 through a series of lectures and in England by the

Society for Pure English, a private group in which the poet Robert Bridges played an important role, through a series of tracts published between 1919 and 1948. In 1978, two writers, Arn and Charlene Tibbetts, in *What's Happening to American English?* proposed setting up an American Society for Good English. The most recent proposal for some kind of academy or authority is in John Honey's 1997 book *Language is Power*. Honey believes that "the time has again arrived to agitate for the creation of an authoritative body to issue advice on the 'correct' use of English – i.e., the most acceptable usages, those which find most favour among educated people." He wants to continue the work of refining standard English and to slow down change. Honey believes that standard English has so much to offer speakers of all varieties of English that it merits this attention.

Following the publication of Johnson's dictionary, others began to produce dictionaries in the Johnsonian tradition. As successive dictionaries were published, they acquired more and more authority and many of their authors' assumptions became "truths' about the language. For example, spelling became increasingly rigid. Johnson had tried to adopt a rational and consistent spelling system, but when we find him using *downhil* alongside *uphill*, *moveable* but *immovable*, *distil* but *instill*, *conceit* but *receipt*, and *interiour* but *exterior*, we see some of the problems that Johnson had with resolving different spellings.

Johnson also expressed his views about pronunciation, preferring the example of "the most elegant speakers who deviate least from the written words"; his models were those he considered to be the best speakers of the language. In the dictionaries that followed Johnson's we can see spelling called more and more into play as a guide to pronunciation. For example, the *New Universal Etymological English Dictionary* produced by Nathaniel Bailey and Joseph Scott in 1755 informs us that: "The pronunciation is true when every letter has its proper sound." John Entick's *The New Spelling Dictionary* of 1765 reminds us that: "In all languages it is necessary, in order to speak and write correctly and properly, to be instructed in the rules for right pronunciation." Other post-Johnsonians like William Kenrick, Thomas Sheridan, and John Walker wanted to establish a permanent standard of pronunciation using spelling as a guide. One of the main objectives of Sheridan's *A General Dictionary of the English Language*, published in 1780, was "to establish a plain and permanent standard of Pronunciation," a phrase taken from its title page.

More than two centuries later we can look back at the eighteenth century and see that little has changed in our attitudes toward dictionaries and language. We regard dictionaries as authoritative and spend little time or effort in trying to assess the sources of this authority. We do not question the labels we find, the preference for one pronunciation or definition of a word over another or others, or the aura of infallability. We find the same need to set one variey of language over others, to exalt the written forms of language far above the spoken forms, to seek for invariance in the face of variety, and to let others do our thinking about language – or what often passes as thinking – for us.

3 Plowing New Fields

Across the Atlantic Noah Webster assumed Johnson's role as a possible "fixer" of the American variety of the language. A trained lawyer but not a practicing one, Webster became an entrepreneur publisher. He saw an opportunity not only to give Americans a certain pride in their language – "to diffuse an uniformity and purity of language," as he said in one of his prefaces – but also to make money while doing so. He became the "schoolmaster to America," producing both dictionaries and spelling books, particularly the famous "blue-backed speller," first published in 1783 and given this name because of its distinctive binding. Some twenty million copies of this speller were sold during Webster's lifetime and well over sixty million copies after his death. However, the speller did not enrich Webster as it might have done because he sold off the various rights for small but immediate amounts of money and he was the victim of poor accounting practices and open piracy. Webster also published grammars, and treatises and essays on a variety of topics, especially on politics, medicine, and religion. One of his religious books was a bowdlerized Bible, a testament to Webster's essentially conservative, puritan, genteel nature.

Webster published his first dictionary in 1806, a small school dictionary of just over 400 pages plus a 24-page preface entitled *A Compendious Dictionary of the English Language*. He followed it with an abridgment in 1807. He defined *compendious* in the dictionary as a "short, brief, concise, summary." This first dictionary contains such spellings as *ax, heater, center, labor, honor, favor, music, logic, disciplin, doctrin, examin, medicin,* and *opake* (with *opaque* included in brackets). Webster also included the words *advisory* and *presidential* and some verbs ending in *-ize* such as *demoralize* and *Americanize* but met with criticism for doing so.

Webster spent much of the next twenty years laboring over *An American Dictionary of the English Language,* which finally emerged in 1828. Like Johnson's dictionary before it, Webster's *American Dictionary* was an amazing piece of work for a single author. One of Webster's goals was to make Americans proud of their language. As he said in his Preface, "The necessity . . . of a Dictionary to the people of the United States is obvious"; he wanted "to furnish an American Work which shall be a guide to the youth of the United States." Since Webster wanted to show where British and American usage differed, he included words of entirely American provenance. He drew widely on American authors such as Benjamin Franklin, George Washington, and Washington Irving for his citations. However, Webster constantly stressed the similarities between American English and British English. He believed that the language provided a strong tie between the two countries and sent Queen Victoria a copy of the second American edition, an edition which was a long time forthcoming because it took thirteen years to sell out the 2500 copies of the first edition.

As early as 1789, in an appendix to his *Dissertations on the English Language*, Webster had expressed a belief that English spelling should be reformed and agreed with Benjamin Franklin in this. However, Franklin, like Shaw more than a century later, wanted a completely new alphabet, an idea Webster rejected. Scorning the "pedantic orthography" of Johnson's dictionary, Webster was determined to provide American English, the "AMERICAN TONGUE" in his words, with a different spelling system from that of British English and, in doing so, make it more consistent and rational. Webster was aware of how reliant Americans had become on spelling as a guide to pronunciation and his solution was to reform spelling. This reform would help bring about uniformity of pronunciation in the new nation, and the new spelling would become part of the new "national language." Webster added: "I am confident that such an event is an object of vast political consequence." A new spelling system would be a source of national pride.

Webster's early works proposed and in some cases incorporated a large number of spellings that were not found in British English. Some of the more radical changes additional to those cited previously were *fateeg* (*fatigue*), *mareen* (*marine*), *bred* (*bread*), *bilt* (*built*), *near* (*neer*), *karacter* (*character*), *korus* (*chorus*), *tuf* (*tough*), *kee* (*key*), *laf* (*laugh*), *blud* (*blood*), *mashine* (*machine*), *filosophy* (*philosophy*), *det* (*debt*), *ritten* (*written*), *giv* (*give*), *speek* (*speak*), *obleek* (*oblique*), *reezon* (*reason*), *iz* (*is*), *acknowlege* (*acknowledge*), *wurds* (*words*), *altho* (*although*), and *ilans* (*islands*). Webster was not consistent in his proposals: whereas *crumb* and *thumb* would become *crum* and *thum*, *dumb* and *limb* would remain as they were. None of the above suggestions, except for some occasional use of *altho*, has been adopted, but a few others, which reformers other than Webster also favored, were, spellings like *honor, center, meter, music, draft, ax, plow, organize, connection*, and *traveled*. Webster was wise enough to acknowledge how difficult it is to change spelling habits. There was considerable opposition to his proposed reforms: people do not willingly change something whose acquisition may have caused them considerable difficulty, and sometimes even physical pain.

Webster wanted to give American English its own flavor. He wanted an American English that would be distinctively different from the British variety – "*A national language* is a brand of *national union* " he declared – but not so different that mutual intelligibility would be lost. However, he failed to change the spelling system in a drastic way. Like all spelling reformers, he had hoped to make that system easier to learn. He had also hoped that his new spellings would capture "good" American pronunciation and bring about a uniform, permanent pronunciation, another ambition common to reformers. In Webster's opinion the best speech in North America was to be found among the American yeomanry, "substantial independent freeholders, masters of their own persons and lords of their own soil," who were therefore quite a cut above the illiterate English peasantry of the time. Only two American pronunciations seem to be clearly ascribable to Webster's work, *lieutenant* and *schedule*; in each case he chose to endorse a pronunciation that differed from the one his British contemporaries endorsed, and Americans followed his choice.

Through his dictionary and spelling books Webster focused attention on the written language and notions of invariance, correctness, and morality. His dictionaries are larded with example sentences extolling the religious, moral, and political values he held: "In many cases, I have given brief sentences of my own and often presenting some important maxim or statement in religion, morality, law or civil policy." Some examples speak clearly to the consequences: "It is the duty, as it is the desire, of a good man to *improve* in grace and piety"; "The *love* of God is the first duty of man"; "We *reverence* superiors for their age, their authority, and their virtues"; "Pay due respect to those who are superior in station, and due civility to those who are *inferior*"; "The privileges of American citizens, civil and religious, are *inestimable*"; and "*Patriotism* is the characteristic of a good citizen, the noblest passion that animates a man in the character of a citizen."

Like Johnson before him, Webster did little to change the language but did influence how people regarded it. His successful spelling innovations were few and the differences between current American and British spelling are minor, but this does not mean for some users of the language that they are unimportant. Because of the success of Johnson's and Webster's dictionaries people have come to look on dictionaries as major sources of authority concerning the language. If a word is not in the dictionary, it is not in the language. Moreover, some words should not be allowed into dictionaries or, if they are allowed, should be clearly labeled as "inferior." A dictionary should tell those who use it what a word "really means," how they "should" use it, and how they "must" pronounce it. A dictionary should not equivocate about what it says on each of these matters because authorities do not equivocate; they judge and pronounce their judgments, and we other mortals obey. Neither Johnson nor Webster thought

his work should be used like this; Johnson knew that it was impossible for a dictionary to fix the language for all time, and
Webster was too aware of his own personal and political agenda
to claim any kind of finality for his work. However, the tradition
we have inherited is largely silent on those aspects of their work
and beliefs.

4 Sabotage in Springfield

Just how important dictionaries had become as sources of authority for the language became apparent with the publication of
Webster's Third in 1961. The only possible explanation of the reaction that followed publication is that by the mid-twentieth century the dictionary had assumed a status rather like that of the
Bible in the eyes of those who had acquired familiarity with print.
The dictionary had become an indespensable guide to "good" linguistic behavior, especially in North America.

The British did not share this view. In England James Murray,
a Scot, had produced the monumental *Oxford English Dictionary*,
or *OED*, to considerable acclaim. It is instructive to compare the
etymologies in the *OED* with those of Webster to see an entirely
different set of goals at work: Murray delving industriously into
the past and Webster relying on intuition and guesswork. The
OED, published between 1884 and 1928, with a first supplement
published in 1933 and a more recent one directed by Robert
Burchfield issued between 1972 and 1986, is a remarkable record
of the development of English vocabulary. The idea for the dictionary had originated in Richard Chenevix Trench's criticism of
existing dictionaries in 1857, "On some deficiencies in our English dictionaries." Trench declared that a dictionary should be a
comprehensive inventory of the standard language that included
all its words and their meanings. It should also provide citations
for the uses it records and scholarly etymologies. A dictionary
should be a historical document not an arbiter of taste. Murray
followed these principles in producing the *OED*.

In contrast to Trench and Murray the American
dictionary-makers were not interested in historical scholarship;

they preferred authority even though they professed a strong belief in democracy. The social and cultural climate in the United States encouraged a desire to remove differences, to focus on the present, and to prepare for the future. Where better to begin than with eliminating differences in the use of language and with improving the language of all those who were so eagerly reaching America's shores? American dictionary-makers and dictionary-users have therefore preferred dictionaries that act as guides to "good language behavior."

What was so devastating to the sensibilities of many Americans in 1961 was that *Webster's Third* attempted to describe the way words were being used in American English rather than tell people how they should use words. The dictionary was 27 years in the making, drew on the knowledge of several hundred scholars, and used as its sources millions of citations taken from the language of the preceding two centuries. *Webster's Third* was not a historical dictionary in the Oxford tradition but one that described the language as it was being used. It tried to be comprehensive and complete. Consequently, it included words not seen before in many American dictionaries, described how words were variously used and pronounced, and avoided moralizing. It used only a few labels to describe words, e.g., "nonstandard" (for words like *irregardless* and the use of *lay* for *lie*), "substandard" (for *ain't, hisself, drownded,* and *youse*), "slang" (for *boondocks, cornball, fuzz, lulu,* and *screw-up*), "vulgar" (for the usual "four-letter" words but not for *damn* or *hell*), and a rare "obscene." These labels were used sparingly and one, "colloquial," used in almost every other dictionary, was not used at all on the grounds that it is meaningless since everybody speaks colloquial English. *Like* was described as both a preposition and a conjunction so that its use in a sentence like *Do it like I say* could be explained rather than condemned. *Webster's Third* drew its quotations from a wide range of sources, including Mickey Spillane, Elizabeth Taylor, Ethel Merman, Polly Adler, Art Linkletter, Pearl Buck, Edith Sitwell, T. S. Eliot, the *Police Gazette*, and the *Marine Corps Manual*.

The dictionary met with a storm of criticism in North America. It was called a "scandal and a disaster" and a "political pamphlet." It was likened to the Kinsey reports of 1948 and 1953 (named after their author Alfred Kinsey) on American sexual behavior as being clearly intended to undermine American morality. It was said to be "bolshevik" in spirit and deliberately subversive of the existing political and social order. Criticism of the dictionary, not all of it as intemperate as this, appeared everywhere: the *Atlantic Monthly*, the *American Scholar*, the *Saturday Review*, the *New Republic*, the journal of the American Bar Association, the *New Yorker*, *Life*, *Business Week*, the *Library Journal*, and newspapers like the *New York Times*, the *Washington Post*, and the *Chicago Tribune*. In contrast, across the Atlantic, the reviews in British publications were generally favorable, the British being more accustomed to the idea that dictionaries should describe rather than prescribe.

Each critic had his own criticisms. Jacques Barzun, a distinguished teacher and scholar, castigated the editors of the dictionary and declared that its faults were apparent with just a "casual glance." Sheridan Baker, a professor of English and author later of *The Complete Stylist*, declared in his presidential address to the Michigan Academy of Science, Arts, and Letters in 1965 that: "Good English has to do with the upper classes – and there's the rub – with the cultural and intellectual leaders." *Webster's Third* had clearly stepped far beyond those bounds. Mario Pei, a Romance philologist who in *Invitation to Linguistics* actually showed his distrust and misunderstanding of linguistics, particularly in its various appendices, blamed that growing science for the "permissiveness" he found in the dictionary and for the its apparent lack of standards.

The critics had a variety of complaints, often quite idiosyncratic ones, but there was widespread agreement on a few points, for example, on the description of *like* as both a preposition and a conjunction, on the inclusion of *ain't* and *irregardless*, and on the recognition that *disinterested* was often used with the meaning of *uninterested*. Few critics bothered to check their facts either about what the previous 1934 edition of the dictionary had said on the points they disputed or the historical record. It was enough that they disagreed with the dictionary and that its editors had preferred to report on the current state of the language rather than issue a set of edicts about it.

According to many critics, certain words should not have been included in the dictionary at all. Some words that were in the dictionary were said to be improperly described, the critics refusing to believe that they were used in the way that the dictionary said that they were used. However, whereas the dictionary could provide evidence to support what it said about these words, the critics could not. The critics complained that there were either no labels describing certain usages or that the labels were too liberal. There should have been an element of proscription in the dictionary achieved either by the deliberate exclusion of certain words or by strong "negative" labeling if they were included. Finally, only the "best" users of the language should have been cited in quotations used in the dictionary because those who use dictionaries need "authorities" they can look up to.

Linguists had a different view of the dictionary; they greeted it very positively. It was also welcomed in the United Kingdom, where the same cult of dictionary worship was far less well developed and people were much more accepting both of language variety and of dictionaries that actually told users how words were used and had been used. They had the example of the *OED* to guide them.

The American critic Wilson Follett went so far as to argue that there had been "sabotage in Springfield," the home city of the publishers of the dictionary. Much of his criticism of the dictionary was misguided, depending on either an ignorance – wilfull or otherwise – of historical facts about the language or applying irrelevant considerations such as logic in discussing whether *center about* should be preferred to *center around*. In his review article in the *Atlantic Monthly*, Follett called the dictionary "a very great calamity," accused its editors of "snap judgments," and proclaimed that the dictionary was a "fighting document." However, he did make an important point: the real problem with *Webster's Third*, he argued, was that it did not give people what they expected from a dictionary. They expect to be told how to use their language when they go to a dictionary. Instead *Webster's Third* told them how their fellow Americans used the language and that is not the same thing. In Follett's view those who publish dictionaries cannot change the rules of dictionary-making like this, a comment that tells us much about the function of dictionaries in people's lives.

We can look at this matter in another way. We cannot fault what *Webster's Third* says about a word like *ain't*. The facts about *ain't* reported there are facts. But how should a dictionary interpret them? Should it report them at all? In the view of Bergen Evans, writing in the *Atlantic Monthly*, a dictionary must report the facts and say something about their status: "Words in themselves are not dignified, or silly, or wise, or malicious. But they can be used in dignified, silly, wise, or malicious ways by dignified, silly, wise, or malicious people." In the view of critics like Follett, if a dictionary includes such words at all, it has an obligation to interpret their uses rather than report them without comment because that is what people expect from a dictionary. Lexicographers are not free to abrogate the authority we have conferred upon them. John Simon echoes these views in *Paradigms Lost*, declaring: "Alas, even the best dictionaries tend to abrogate [their] authority" and adding that people like himself must use even the *OED* "with discrimination." According to Simon, dictionaries must "lay down the law about what is right and wrong" and "if a dictionary does not lay down the law about what is right and what is wrong . . . who will?" But then, by Simon's own admission, "looking up things in dictionaries has become important to me."

However, this laying down of language law is quite problematic. Who should lay it down? How are we to choose our masters? Most of those who have tried to lay down such law without writing dictionaries have been self-appointed to the task. Those who have actually written dictionaries like Johnson, Webster, and Murray found the experience humbling when it came to trying to be authoritative about how the language should be used rather than about how it is used. If the editors of a dictionary decide to lay down the law, what kinds of evidence should they look for as they go about their work? The large, unabridged dictionaries produce masses of evidence for what they say. Is there something wrong about such evidence, or should some of it be ruled inadmissible? And if so, on what grounds?

Linguists believe that a dictionary of a language should tell us how people use that language at a particular time and in a particular place. Once we have a good description of such use it is up to individuals to decide how to use that description. If for some reason people want to advise others about *ain't, irregardless, disinterested, drownded,* and the use of *like* as a conjunction, they must first of all be sure of their facts. A dictionary should tell them what these facts are. What they do with them is their business, not the business of the dictionary. However, this is not the attitude that many people have toward a dictionary. The controversy over *Webster's Third* amply demonstrated that fact. For their part though, linguists must recognize how dictionaries fit into a set of beliefs about what a language is. They cannot ignore these beliefs or dismiss them as unworthy of comment. We must also recognize that trying to change people's beliefs about dictionaries will be an extremely difficult task.

This is not an issue that is likely to go away. Today we have dictionaries of many kinds published for many different reasons. Some have explicit agendas: for example, various feminist dictionaries designed either to make us aware of "sexist" language or to persuade us to eliminate such language from use. But agendas have long been a part of dictionary-making. Johnson, Webster, and Murray each had an agenda.

There is also a certain circularity in much dictionary-making. For example, if there must be a written citation for each entry in a dictionary, how do we represent the spoken language, and how do we not bias the dictionary toward literary sources, the creators of that literature, and those who edit what is written? Editors, particularly copy editors, are our language gate-keepers. How much stronger would the dictionary evidence be for the widespread use of *irregardless, like* as a preposition, the split infinitive, *flaunt* for *flout,* and so on if spoken sources and unedited prose were used more widely? It is difficult to see how any dictionary can be entirely "objective" no matter however strong the claims that are made for it.

5 Don't Tell it Like it is

One immediate result of the publication of *Webster's Third* was that another publisher attempted to buy it out so that the dictionary could be suppressed as "an affront to scholarship." This attempt failed so the publisher decided to give the public – or that vocal segment of the public that had protested so vehemently – what it apparently wanted, a dictionary that spoke with authority. The *American Heritage Dictionary of the English Language* was launched with great fanfare in 1969; it would repair the sabotage done in Springfield.

This dictionary was designed to give its readers guidance in their use of the language. The publisher decided that the editors needed a panel of experts to help them in their work so that the dictionary could offer its users "the lexical opinions of a large group of highly sophisticated fellow citizens." This panel, originally 94 men and eleven women, consisted of writers, critics, historians judges, editors, professors of various subjects, and educators; however, scholars whose specialty was linguistics or the history of the language were not welcome. The panel also included published critics of *Webster's Third*, people like Jacques Barzun, Dwight McDonald, and Mario Pei. (Later, in *Paradigms Lost*, John Simon called the members of this panel "a catholic but not consistently compelling lot." You cannot please everybody!)

According to one of the editors of the *American Heritage Dictionary*, the panelists deliberately "eschewed the 'scientific delusion' that a dictionary should contain no value judgments." So value judgments there were aplenty in the resulting work! The dictionary included usage notes for 226 entries covering 318 points altogether. *Irregardless* was excluded from consideration: it had no place in this dictionary.

What is particularly interesting is the amount of disagreement among the panel members and the idiosyncratic nature of their opinions. There was almost unanimous disapproval of some words and usages, e.g., of *ain't*, *between you and I*, *thusly*, and *flaunt* with the meaning of *flout*. On the other hand, there was nearly unanimous approval for *drop out* used as a noun, *slow* used as an adverb, and *anxious* used in the sense of *eager*. Somewhere between there was majority rejection (and therefore minority acceptance) of *bus* and *loan* as verbs, *alibi* used in the sense of *excuse*, *most everyone*, *in back of*, *finalize*, *rather unique*, and *try* followed by *and*.

The use of such a panel revealed that people with conservative and often very loudly expressed views about the language cannot agree among themselves on many of the controversial points. The panel has changed both its personnel and its opinions over time. Geoffrey Nunberg's 1990 paper, "What the Usage Panel Thinks," showed that by 1988 its views had become more "liberal." It was more accepting than in 1969 of the use of *anxious* in the sense of *eager*, *aggravating* in the sense of *irritating*, and *decimate* as meaning "almost wiped out." However, it overwhelmingly rejected the use of *hopefully* as a sentence adverb and *disinterested* with the meaning of *uninterested*, and resisted any possibility of modifying *unique* – some defences are not to be breached! Nunberg himself writes "none of these usages were any less common twenty years ago than now" whereas most – possibly all – of those who were critical of *Webster's Third* would have insisted on *was* for *were* in that comment.

William and Mary Morris employed a similar panel to resolve controversies for their *Harper Dictionary of Contemporary Usage* of 1975. They sought the opinions of "136 writers, editors, and public speakers" on certain controversial, linguistic matters. These authorities were asked to state the reasons for their judgments. Once again we find an enormous variety of opinions and little concern for facts. The panel showed a greater degree of tolerance for variety in the spoken language than in the written language. Its members were nearly unanimous in proscribing *between you and I*, *irregardless*, and *disinterested* meaning *uninterested*, although they did accept *It's me*. However, what confidence can we have in usage judgments expressed in terms like *damnable, barbaric, vile, horrible, sloppy, illiterate*, and *makes me physically sick*?

Other polls and surveys about usage conducted on both sides of the Atlantic continue to produce similar results, i.e., wide areas of agreement and disagreement. In a study entitled *Attitudes to English Usage*, published in 1970, which reported on a survey in England among teachers at different levels of education, W. H. Mittins and his co-workers found considerable censoriousness. They asked the teachers to rate 55 usages for degrees of approval and disapproval in formal and informal speech and writing, e.g., *aggravate*, *compared to* rather than *compared with*, and sentences ending with prepositions. The teachers were willing to do this task and volunteered additional examples of usages of which they disapproved. However, there were wide differences of opinion regarding the 55 items surveyed. There was majority approval, i.e., more favorable than unfavorable reposes in all circumstances, for *averse to*, *data* followed by *is*, the use of *each other* and *between* for more than two, and *either* followed by more than one use of *or*. There was majority disapproval of the following items, given here in decreasing order of approval, i.e., the least approved last: misplaced *only*, *due to* (*because of*), *He is older than me*, *different to*, *these sort of plays*, *try and arrive*, *told Charles and I*, *like* as a conjunction or with a meaning eqivalent to *as though*, *loan* for *lend*, the use of "dangling" participles, *imply* with the meaning of *infer*, and *very unique*, this last with 89 percent disapproval.

In *Language is Power* John Honey touches on matters of "correctness." He deplores what has happened to the meanings of *decimate*, *reticent*, and *cohort*, and a common failure to distinguish the meanings of *may have* and *might have*. He expresses tolerance of *for you and I* and favors the adoption of a third person singular, unisex pronoun. In matters of pronunciation he strongly disapproves of glottalization in Estuary English, i.e., pronouncing word final *t's* as glottal stops. He is also firm in his condemnation of the medial flapped *t* in American pronunciation, e.g. the pronunciation of the middle consonant of *butter*. Honey claims that *writer* and *rider* and *bitten* and *bidden* are difficult to distinguish (they are not): "Some features of American English . . . deserve to be resisted by anyone concerned for intelligibility and clear communication." Since Honey is in favor of establishing an "authoritative body" to provide advice to those who use English, we can only wonder how much agreement he would find in such a body for his views on these items.

What we just seen is considerable concern being expressed about, and considerable effort being expended on, a small set of usages in the language. Moreover, those who express such concern do not always agree among themselves about how "proper" or "improper" each item is. Their opinions are always personal opinions buttressed not by facts but by claims about what the author of a particular opinion regards as logical, clear, precise, or pure in the language on the one hand, or barbaric, slovenly, corrupt, or offensive on the other.

The opinions voiced do change – slowly however – over time, because those voicing them realize that they have "lost the battle" or that language change is inevitable. Nevertheless, we cannot ignore the fact that certain language uses have become shibboleths so far as the taste-makers and gate-keeepers of many of our cultural and literary traditions are concerned. For such people, particularly useful shibboleths are split infinitives, *hopefully* used as a sentence adverb, *Drive slow*, *different* followed by *than* rather than *from*, *It's me*, *ain't*, *alibi* with the meaning of *excuse*, the "confusion" of *imply* and *infer*, and the use of *like* as a conjunction. For many the "health" of the English language, the study of its grammar, and any ideas of "correctness" have become reduced to this kind of trivial pursuit: avoiding a particular word here or another one there. We do not know why we must behave like this, only that we must. The facts of usage, as these are reported in *Webster's Dictionary of English Usage* of 1989, are largely hidden from view. Facts are deemed to be irrelevant for only opinions count, with some opinions counting more than others.

These opinions concerning "correct English" do, however, have a social reality we cannot ignore. We can see how the 1997 *Guide to Canadian English* tries to recognize this reality. The guide is published by the Strathy Language Unit of Queen's University in Canada, an academic enterprise endowed by a businessman J. R. Strathy, who founded the unit "to promote the use of correct English in Canada and to produce a usage guide for Canadians." However, this is what Fee and McAlpine have to say in their introduction to the book they produced: "Usage conventions arise precisely in areas where choice is possible, and though usage guides are expected to approve one choice as 'correct' and others as 'incorrect,' sloppy, or vulgar, this guide – perhaps to the frustration of some readers – is more likely to lay out the possibilities and to discuss the contexts where different choices might be effective." Does such a statement reveal a failure to give people – including Mr Strathy – what they want? Is it therefore an abdication of responsibility? Or is it just common sense?

6 One Standard or Various Standards?

English is now a well standardized language, that is, there is wide-spread agreement about most of its features and a considerable apparatus exists to reinforce such agreement: an extensive literature, dictionaries, grammars, guide books, style manuals, editorial practices, and so on. However, the agreement is not an absolute one and a considerable circularity underlies the whole process with dictionaries, grammars, and guide books, which are largely based on literary sources, constraining editors, who in turn constrain writers, and so on. There are also local standards associated with countries as distant from one another as the United Kingdom, the United States, South Africa, and Australia, and, though more controversially, India, Nigeria, Singapore, and Kenya, where the local varieties of English receive mixed reactions.

However, there is no fixed standard of English pronunciation. Some people believe that Received Pronunciation (or RP) is such a standard within England, but standard English is not tied to any particular accent. In his prefatory remarks to the first edition of his *English Pronouncing Dictionary* Daniel Jones, the famous English phonetician, said that he was presenting no more than "a faithful record of the manner in which certain people *do* pronounce" the language rather than should pronounce it. He added: "I take the view that people should be allowed to speak as they like." His words went largely unheeded. For example, Henry Wyld, an Oxford philologist, declared in 1934 that RP represented "the best kind of English" because the "best people" used it and, in his view, it was noteworthy for what he described as the "clarity of its sounds." It was in Wyld's opinion, the "most pleasing and sonorous form" of the language and officers of the British Regular Army best exemplified its use, because it gave perfect expression to their manliness, lack of affectation, and urbanity. It was the accent of the upper reaches of academia, army and naval officers, the Anglican Church, the highest courts of law, and the senior civil service. It was the accent of power and this fact was known to the powerful and powerless alike.

RP is a very important English accent although it is perhaps not as invariant today as it was just a half century ago. It is a clear social marker in the United Kingdom. As George Steiner says in *After Babel*, "Upper-class English diction, with its sharpened vowels, elisions, and modish slurs, is both a code for mutual recognition – accent is worn like a coat of arms – and an instrument of ironic exclusion." I am not so sure about "ironic" in that observation; it never struck me that way. (Steiner also remarks on "the thick twilight of Cockney speech" – nothing ironic there!) Speakers with RP accents always use standard English, but many users of standard English do not have RP accents, and nonstandard users never use RP. These three language groupings also correspond very closely with social groupings and with all the latter entails.

In *Does Accent Matter?*, a discussion of accents in England, John Honey answers his own question as follows: "Children should be warned to expect in the real world their accents may be used as an indicator of their origins, the extent of their educatedness, the system of values with which they identify and whether these are associated with a narrow local group or with the wider society." Such stereotyping is important and that these are bold words. However, Honey also believes that some accents are intrinsically better than others. How else can we interpret his comment that "the English language is a treasure trove of precious things whose beauty can, at least in some degree, be measured in the way they are spoken"?

Both standard English and RP achieved their position not because of any intrinsic values they had. Some variety of the language was not "better" than any other variety and therefore inevitably became the standard. Nor was one accent inherently better than others. It is impossible to say what "better" or "worse" could mean in such a context. The variety of English that we now refer to as standard English achieved its position by accident. It was the variety of the language that a powerful group in society used at a time when it was desirable to promote that variety in order to consolidate power. If, as John Marenbon declares in *English our English*, "Standard English is the language of English culture at its highest levels as it has developed over the last centuries," that linguistic triumph is entirely a political and social one. However, it is no less real for that. Such an observation is not an attack on standard English; it is simply a clarification of what happened.

At some point in time one variety of a languge comes through a particular combination of circumstances – usually political but not always – to represent that language best. People are required to give conscious attention to it and begin to describe its characteristics in grammars and dictionaries. The variety is used in many different circumstances, particularly in the affairs of state, in religious worship, and in the "better" types of literature. It becomes the variety that is taught in the schools. Some people become highly protective of it. The variety is now "official" – either *de facto* or *de jure* – and becomes a standard language.

The standard is always a kind of ideal that people have for the language, a homogenized and artificial creation. It is possibly a necessary ideal for such domains as administration, law, education, and literature. No one person or even one group of persons was resposible for it. Certainly, those who wrote the dictionaries and grammars associated with it were not; they just helped it along. As Hans von Jagemann said in his presidential address to the Modern Language Association in 1899, "That the weather clerk really makes the weather probably none but infants believe, but that language is made by compilers of dictionaries and grammars is a conception not confined to the young or ignorant." Furthermore, there is no ideal speaker.

The ideal is an abstraction; the language itself varies from place to place and from person to person. It also exists in both spoken forms and written forms, which may not agree. In daily use the language must inevitably fail to live up to the ideal, which is also a "frozen," inflexible one. Ideals are not easy things to live up to in a real world of change and differences. The ideal that is held before us does make us conscious of language; however, the language we use every day is habitual, more closely resembling what we do when we breathe or walk than what we do when we calculate our taxes or play chess. Our everyday language is often a nonstandard dialect and therein lies a serious problem for many: just how should we relate the one to the other?

Standard English exists as both as an ideal and as a set of practices supported by people Deborah Cameron calls "craft professionals" in *Verbal Hygiene*. We have an alphabet and we have a principle of alphabetical order: these took many centuries to work out. There is a considerable uniformity in spelling conventions with some differences between North America and the rest of the English-using world (with many Canadians not really knowing where they "live" in this regard). The grammar of the language is much the same everywhere. That is, after all, why we can discuss something called "English": it could not exist without a massive sharing of knowledge of its characteristics among those who either use it or recognize it. However, we do not always agree on a few of these characteristics, and this disagreement can become contentious. We also have conventions for printing and writing the language, for punctuation, and so on. There is fairly widespread agreement too that standard English is the appropriate variety of the language for higher education.

We all believe that there does exist something we can call standard English. In *The Quark and the Jaguar* Murray Gell-Mannn explains the importance of belief as follows: "An organized belief system, complete with myths, may motivate compliance with codes of conduct and cement the bonds uniting the members of a society." That is exactly what standard English does for us, myths and all: it bonds us. If, as Stephen Pinker says in *The Language Instinct*, "It is just common sense that people should be given every encouragement and opportunity to learn the dialect that has become the standard one in their society and to employ it in many formal settings," they will almost certainly learn all the asociated myths about language too.

7 Is it *it's* or *its*?

Many arbitrary decisions have been made during the process of standardization often about trivial matters and without any consistency. Once "decided" though each matter is "fixed." We must never underestimate how important a trivial issue can become to those who hold strongly to ideals. People die for trivialities.

The apostrophe has a variety of uses, which are not easy to master because they are not at all logical: why is there an apostrophe in *John's* but not in *theirs*? Many people know that there are different uses for the apostrophe but never succeed in sorting them out. A restaurant lists *todays' specials*, another advises us that *Tobys say's . . .*, a store informs its customers that it sells *coffee's and tea's*, and another that it is *Open Sunday's*, a vendor sells *peach's* from a truck, an educational institution labels adjacent doors *Ladies* and *Men's*, a hairdresser's is called *Concept's*, a hat store *Hat's Galore*, and a children's clothing store *Kid's*. A television show tells us in a printed message flashed across the screen that *Madonna's new video is pushing the industry to it's limits*, and in *The Letters of John Cheever*, we find that John Cheever, winner of both the National Book Award and the Pulitzer Prize, appears to have written *it's* for *its* and *their's* for *theirs* throughout his life.

The problem with the apostrophe is not just a modern one. In the eighteenth century Joseph Priestley observed, without comment, uses such as *toga's* and *idea's* among his contemporaries. In the nineteenth century we find examples like *fly's, railway station's*, and *opera's* cited in Henry Alford's *The Queen's English* of 1864, usages Alford describes as "curious." Such uses are just as curious today in their persistence.

If we did not have an apostrophe in the written language, what would we lose? Probably very little. The best advice to students seems to be: "When in doubt leave it out," because the sin of omission, i.e., leaving it out when the standard, written language requires it, seems more easily pardoned than the sin of commission, i.e., putting it in when it is not required. The apostrophe will probably be around for a long time (in spite of *Chambers English Dictionary, Barclays Bank, Lloyds Bank*, and *Teachers College* of Columbia University), and endless hours will be spent teaching students how to use it properly in writing, but the end result will still be that apostrophes are scattered around like rice or confetti at a wedding.

We are not alone in experiencing such difficulties. The French spent a lot of energy at the end of the 1980s trying to decide on the future of the circumflex accent. When the High Commission on the French Language finally decided in 1990 to curtail its uses, from the reactions of some of the opponents of the decision you might have thought that it was selling baguettes that was to be restricted in French life rather than using circumflex accents! But what would written French be like without circumflex acents? Or written English without apostrophes?

We see in these cases how difficult it is to change a minor feature in the language once that feature has become established in such a way that it can be used to distinguish among users of the language. If we know and observe the traditional rules for using apostrophes and circumflex accents, we can feel superior to those who lack this knowledge. We can accuse them of ignorance, even of laziness. We can use language to classify people and to assert some kind of superiority. That the particular linguistic point is inconsequential is of little concern; in fact, it is quite irrelevant. The real issue is who gets to control others and say what should and should not be. As Humpty Dumpty construes the problem, who gets to be master? Who gets to play Prospero and who must settle for the role of Caliban?

Not Knowing your Grammar

People react in various ways when they find they are talking to someone who studies language professionally. A typical defensive reaction is: "Oh, I'll have to watch what I say now." Another is to take the opportunity to complain about some bit of "bad grammar" they have noticed. However, the majority assume that there is little of any real interest to discuss: English grammar is pretty much cut and dried after all. It is what is in those dull books that some of them had to work their way through in school; or it is something teachers tried to drill into them; and really the less said about it the better! Any further discussion usually leads to some kind of statement that they do not really have any knowledge of grammar at all, while, naturally, declaring this fact in perfectly grammatical English. Such confusion is not surprising: most of us lack any understanding of how our language works or of the different uses of the words *grammar* and *rules*.

1 Putting Your Best Foot Forward

We can look at the problem of what grammars and rules are in another way. The King James Bible contains sentences such as *But whom say ye that I am?*, *Thy rod and thy staff they comfort me*, and *Surely goodness and mercy shall follow me all the days of my life*, the first with an interesting *whom*, the second with a redundant *they*, and the last with *shall* rather than *will*. Many grammar books describe these usages as "ungrammatical," declaring that *whom* should be *who, they* should be omitted, and *shall* should be *will*. The Bible also uses *like* as a conjunction, another use the grammars prohibit. Who is "right" here, the Bible or the grammars. But what does it mean to be right?

Does using *like* in the Bible in this way and describing it in a dictionary as both a preposition and a conjunction "pressure" people to use it as a conjunction? Wilson Follett said that it did in his diatribe "Sabotage in Springfield." According to Follett, that "darling of advanced libertarians, *like* as a conjunction" is a "regional colloquialism, a rarely seen aberration among competent writers, or an artificially cultivated irritant among defiant ones." In this view dictionaries and grammars deliberately subvert the language when they tell us how people use it.

We might ask whether the historical development of the language has any place in decision-making about what can and should be said in a dictionary or in a grammar. We know that *like* has been used as a conjunction in English for centuries; we cannot ignore this fact because a few influential people claim that it should be used only as a preposition. Our current use of *It's me* is also the result of a long historical development in the language. In *American English Grammar*, Charles Fries explained how *I it am* in Old English changed slowly into *It am I*, then into *It is I*, and finally into the *It's me* of Modern English. The historical development of English shows a clear progression in the use of the subject forms of personal pronouns before verbs and the object forms after them, except in questions like *Who is he?*, which continue to retain the subject form. *It is I*, therefore, has become an anachronism in the language. (This is not to say that this principle applies everywhere in the language today. It does not, as the currency of expressions such as *between you and I* and *Me and my mother went* testifies.)

We should be cautious about arguments that draw heavily on logic in order to decide matters of grammatical rule. Logically, you should not be able to put your best foot forward – unlesss, of course, you have three feet! Are dangling modifiers illogical? In a book on language published by a reputable press, Susie Tucker's *Protean Shape*, we find: "Looking back, it may give us a salutary jolt to see forerunners of our worse selves in various eighteenth-century pillories." Is this sentence illogical and ungrammatical because it contains a participial phrase that "dangles"? If it is, why is a sentence such as *Considering his age, it's remarkable what he can do* not likewise condemnned? What we are dealing with here is another issue, the special rules of heavily edited prose, which we break on occasion.

When we do find people talking about grammatical rules, they are the rules that people are required to observe in writing heavily edited prose. We are also supposed to try to make our spoken language conform to these rules. This requirement leads many to say that they do not know their grammar. They are saying that they do not know this set of rules for prose but then few of us aspire to be copy editors. They may be aware that they do not follow these rules when they speak, having been told this often enough and made to feel uncomfortable about it. Consequently, they may tell you that their speech is ungrammatical. However, it is perfectly grammatical in the sense that it is always consistent in the rules that it does follow. Stephen Pinker makes this point about the rule-following ability of ordinary speakers of the language rather well in *The Language Instinct*: "common people, no matter how poorly educated, obey sophisticated grammatical laws, and can express themselves with a vigor and grace that captivates those who listen seriously – linguists, journalists, oral historians, novelists with an ear for dialogue." However, these rules – grammatical laws for Pinker – are different from, but really not much different from, the rules of the edited, written variety. The differences are enough to create endless misunderstandings about the notions of grammars and rules. We should, therefore, not be surprised that John Simon can tell us in *Paradigms Lost* that: "Grammar is a tricky, inconsistent thing." It is so because most of us have no clear understanding of what we mean when we use the term *grammar*.

The BBC can, in its *The Spoken Word*, try to ban from the air *There's two, everyone* followed by plural verbs, *data* used as a singular, *between you and I*, and *like* used as a conjunction, and insist on the use of *less money* but *fewer people*, while at the same time showing some tolerance for *who* instead of *whom*, *different than* as well as *different from*, the splitting of infinitives, the placement of *only* somewhat distant from what it modifies, and *none* followed by *are*. It can do this, and insist on doing it, because those who control the airwaves say that that is how English should be used rather than how it is used. English grammar is what they say it is rather than what we might observe it to be. Those who treat grammar like this do not concern themselves with most of the rules of the language; they are not even aware of them. They insist on prescribing a few arbitrary rules that we are required to follow or suffer social consequences. These few rules become the "grammar" we concern ourselves with and the great many uncontroversial rules we all follow are ignored completely. And many of us become willing participants in this conspiracy whose only victims are ourselves.

2 Language Through a Looking-Glass

We look at language the way we do because, as in many other aspects of western life and culture today, we have drawn our ideas from those who lived in Greece, Rome, and the territories controlled by Greeks and Romans in the centuries just before and after the birth of Christ. It is to these peoples that we owe much of our grammatical terminology and many of our ideas about language. It is because their languages – particularly Latin – persisted for centuries and exerted such an influence through their written forms that we have acquired our beliefs about what languages are "really like," beliefs that have helped mold our views of later-emerging vernaculars such as English and French. We cannot escape the influence of Greek and Roman thought when we talk about English, although we may not be conscious of this fact.

Because of the settlement history of Greece, the nature of the terrain, and the system of political organization that evolved, the language of ancient Greece was not a uniform language like – a conjunction here, but would *as* be such a great improvement? – standard English is today. Greek was a language made up of different dialects, and specific dialects became associated with specific uses and with specific kinds of literature. What today we call classical Greek is the particular dialect in which such works as the *Iliad* and the *Odyssey* were composed within a strong oral rather than written tradition.

The Greeks were much interested in language just as they were interested in any number of things, and in the fifth and fourth centuries BCE they debated many linguistic issues. Two key ones were whether language was natural or conventional and whether or not languages were "regular." Much Greek interest in language was therefore philosophical in nature rather than empirical. To-day, many who concern themselves with language would rather speculate about issues than get down to the more serious busi-ness of checking out their claims in detail.

This speculative, philosophical interest among the Greeks found itself united with another interest in rhetoric, the art of persua-sion, an important art in an early democracy of sorts. It also found itself combined with the study of literature because the Greeks cherished the literature they had developed. Along with that lit-erature they had developed a sophisticated writing system so they could ponder how best to preserve what they had thought and written for the benefit of others, both those in their contempo-rary Hellenized world and those who would come after them.

As the Greek world expanded, for example through the con-quests of Alexander the Great in the fourth century BCE, the Greeks developed a description, or grammar, of their language in order to teach Greek to non-Greeks and give them access to their literature. The Alexandrians began the habit of looking back to an earlier, more golden age; they were the first "classicists." The most famous Greek grammar was that of Dionysius Thrax, his *Téchnē*, written in the second century BCE (and still used in Merchant Taylors' School in England in the nineteenth century). In this brief grammar of fifteen pages Thrax, who was interested in the language of poets and writers – "Grammar is the practical knowledge of the general usages of poets and prose writers" – and who drew ultimately on the ideas of Aristotle, describes Greek as having eight parts of speech: noun (with ad-jective a sub-class of the noun class because of its inflectional similarity), verb, participle, article, pronoun, preposition, adverb, and conjunction.

In defining these parts of speech, Thrax used the same criteria we find today in grammars that purport to describe English; some-times inflectional, e.g., many English nouns have different forms for singular and plural; sometimes semantic, e.g., English nouns may be said to name things and verbs to name actions or states, but we must ask ourselves what exactly are "things," "actions," and "states"; and sometimes distributional, e.g., a conjunction joins two clauses. Thrax defined a Greek noun as "a part of a sentence having case inflections, signifying a person or a thing" and a sentence as "a combination of words that have a complete meaning in themselves." His grammar also placed heavy emphasis on parsing, i.e., on naming and classifying words and combinations of words, another tradition that has come down to us along with the names themselves, such as *noun, verb,* and *conjunction.*

The grammar that Thrax wrote is a grammar of Greek words; it almost completely ignores syntax. (Appollonius Dyscolus in the second century CE did, however, supplement Thrax's observations with comments about Greek syntax.) That is another view of language that we have inherited from the Greeks. For large numbers of people, grammar is assigning words to the different parts-of-speech classes, and syntax is not at all important. (Perhaps it does not even exist; English is often described as a language with little or no syntax!)

Other terminology used to describe languages comes from the Greek preoccupation with rhetoric. Sentences are defined in terms of their being statements, questions, or commands, as loose or periodic, and as simple, compound, or complex. Clauses are related to each other on the basis of such principles as equality, concession, reason, and temporalness. It is to Thrax that we owe the definition of the sentence as an expression of "complete meaning" (or in some other translations "complete thought"), a phrase that has bedeviled generations of students and led to untold hours of philosophical discussion. However, the Greeks thought that they needed such terminology if they were to be able to appreciate their literature fully, win arguments in a society that prized rhetorical skills, and be a strong influence in the rest of the world known to them.

The Romans, quintessentially a practical people, limited themselves to taking on the mantle of Greek culture and interests. Except for the odd person like Varro in the first century BCE, who in *De lingua Latina* showed some independence of thought in language matters, they simply took over what the Greeks had said about Greek, translated it, and applied the translations to Latin: beliefs, findings, controversies, categories, and so on. If what they took did not quite fit, then they made it fit one way or another. To be educated in Rome required that you know Greek. The Romans also took over the same Greek interests in literature and rhetoric, and the cornerstone of their educational system became the trivium, the arts of rhetoric, logic, and grammar, with rhetoric at the very center but with grammar providing the entry point. Eventually the pursuit of rhetorical excellence came to be an end in itself in Rome.

The rhetorical tradition in Rome is perhaps best exemplified in the work of Quintilian in the first century. In the twelve books of *Institutio oratoria*, a great educational treatise, Quintilian pointed out the importance of *"recte loquendi scientia"* (the science of correct expression) by which he meant that a Roman should pronounce his language correctly, avoid errors, and be able to parse individual words. He advocated *"bene dicendi scientia"* (the science of good speech), i.e., the art of persuasion, not, as Aristotle conceived this art, as an end in itself, but as a means to good ends. In his comments on the grammatical part of his program, Quintilian showed that he was aware that languages kept changing, that the grammar of Latin differed from that of Greek, and that there was some controversy concerning how many parts of speech there were. (The Romans abandoned the article and replaced it with the interjection, which had been for the Greeks a sub-class of the adverb. Later they dropped the participle and replaced it with the adjective. But the idea that there were eight parts altogether held!) Quintilian believed that the usage of educated people set the standard for the language, what he called *"consensus eruditorium "* (the agreed practice of educated men). But since you were educated only if you had followed the program that Quintilian himself had set out, there was a considerable circularity in that definition.

The two best known Roman grammarians were Donatus in the fourth century and Priscian in the early sixth. They were not original thinkers, but simply applied what they had learned about Greek to Latin, just as in later centuries others would apply what they had learned about Latin from Donatus and Priscian to languages like French and English. Donatus wrote a grammar, his *Ars grammatica*, which stressed such matters as the connection between letters and sounds, the importance of the eight parts of speech, the need to avoid barbarisms, solecisms, and other mistakes, and the use of rhetorical devices. The grammar is mainly concerned with labeling and classifying. "Knowing one's grammar" is knowing what to call each word in the language and knowing how to use words to achieve various effects. The *Institutiones grammaticae* of Priscian, who was a teacher of Greek, was an exhaustive, reference grammar with long lists of words and the changes that could occur in them, observations about exceptions, and illustrations of uses from famous authors. Both grammarians looked back to a golden age for Latin, to the time of writers such as Livy, Virgil, and Cicero. Both used literary works as their sources and ignored the idiomatic prose of Cicero's letters, preferring to describe only the "high style" characteristic of his "literary" writings.

These grammars, particularly Priscian's, with attendant commentaries and glosses became the standard works not only on Latin but on language itself. They established a tradition of language study that exists till this day. After the revival of learning in Europe in the twelfth century, Greek ideas were reintroduced from Arabic, mainly through Spain. Thirteenth-century scholars like Robert Grosseteste and Roger Bacon were responsible for reviving an interest in classical Latin, and Aristotle's influence spread rapidly. Latin became a subject of instruction and was extensively taught as a foreign language. In medieval Europe grammatical study focused almost entirely on the study of Latin. It served all the learned professions of the time, particularly the Church. Whereas the Greeks and the Romans had been interested in many different issues, the Church was interested only in salvation. The study of Latin therefore became almost entirely a vocational study, and students did not ask questions but accepted what they were told.

There was, however, one noticeable exception. A group of grammarians called the Modistae, or speculative grammarians, principally Thomas of Erfurt, at the University of Paris between 1250 and 1320 tried to investigate the relationship of words to reality and whether or not language could be said to mirror the mind or reflect reality. These speculative Aristotelians accepted that Latin best illustrated universal properties of the human mind. They could not free themselves from Latin as they tried to decide what essential grammatical categories logic required that all languages should have.

Given the importance of the Church in medieval life, we might have expected that Hebrew would also have been an important language. However, it was not until the Renaissance that any attention was given to Hebrew within the Semitic tradition the Arabic grammarians had developed. The tradition that language study must be associated with the study of Latin was so long and well established by this time that it remained – and still remains – largely unchallenged.

3 Learning Your English Grammar from the Roots

The tradition that only Latin has a grammar is a long one. It goes back at least two thousand years and was not seriously challenged when people began to write grammars for various vernacular languages. Latin had enormous prestige in the West. It had spread widely, it had left a great literature, and it was the language of the Church, law, medicine, and all learning. Latin had a stranglehold on western thinking about language.

It still does. Philip Howard writes in his Introduction to *Winged Words* as follows: "An English man or woman without Latin is always a stranger in his or her culture and the culture of the West. The best way to learn grammar is from the roots and the nursery, in Latin, and, if you are lucky, Greek." John Marenbon voices similar sentiments, claiming that "standard English has been shaped by Latin usage and by the understanding of grammar involved in a classical education. The traditional, classically-based grammatical categories have themselves influenced the way educated men have spoken and written. . . . the terminology of traditional grammar remains the best instrument for describing the broad features of standard English, and so of prescribing usage to those learning it." In writing like this, Howard and Marenbon are echoing others who believe that English is just another form of Latin, usually a debased form, or that Latin provides us with a universal model of language description. Influential "English" grammar books are sometimes little more than accounts of English as though it were Latin.

It is absurd that anyone can seriously assume that the grammar of Latin, a defunct literary language of an educated elite of two millennia ago, should determine how we must go about providing a coherent account of modern English or of any other language. It is as though we were expected to base a modern zoology entirely on inspections of the cave paintings of animals and speculations about what the painters were thinking about at the time. We are asked to be proud of our ignorance and scornful of recent scientific advances. That is just the recommendation we are being given when we are told to draw exclusively on descriptions of Latin in order to understand how English works.

The earliest grammars of the vernaculars could not escape the influence of Latin nor could we expect them to do so. The Latinate tradition was the only one available to scholars. They therefore drew exclusively on it in describing their own languages. As Ian Michael tells us in *English Grammatical Categories and the Tradition to 1800*, to the early grammarians of the vernaculars Latin "grammar was not just one grammar out of many: it *was* grammar. There could be no question of 'applying Latin' grammar to English. If Latin 'had' a grammar, it was not for English to have anything different. It could have only the same, and less of it." Providing a vernacular with a grammar that made that vernacular resemble Latin would give it the legitimacy of being a "real" language and bring a feeling of pride to those who used it.

At first there was no great need for grammars of the emerging vernaculars because these languages had none of the prestige of Latin. However, a few such grammars were written, e.g., grammars of French, Provençal, Catalan, Italian, and Spanish. Backed by glossaries and manuals of various kinds, these mainly pedagogical grammars were designed to help people who did not speak these languages learn them. For example, the *Donait françois* commissioned by John Barton at the beginning of the fifteenth century, with its goal the teaching of French to speakers of English, relied heavily on Latin sources, particularly the work of Donatus. These grammars tended to focus on writing, spelling, and correct pronunciation. In some cases their authors believed that the vernaculars they were attempting to describe had few rules because the only things they were prepared to treat as "rules" were any resemblances to Latin they could find.

An occasional scholar recognized that this Latinate grammatical apparatus was not entirely perfect. As Vivian Law reminds us in "Language and Its Students: the History of Linguistics," scholars such as Leon Battista Alberti in Italy and Johannes Claius in Germany in the fifteenth and sixteenth centuries were lonely voices in pointing out that Italian and German far from being without rules had their own rules, which differed from those found in Latin.

As the known world expanded during the Renaissance more and more languages came to the attention of western scholars. Many of these languages were very different from those previously known. They included languages from China and other parts of Asia, Sanskrit from India, and a number of languages from the New World, including Quechua from Peru and Guaraní from Brazil. Latinate grammars were written for some of these, but another great interest was in showing how the Lord's Prayer might appear in each. In 1555 Conrad Gesner's *Mithridates* included the prayer in 22 such languages and by 1806 J. C. Adelung's *Mithridates* had expanded that number to more than a thousand examples.

This interest in other languages grew and with it grew the Procrustean exercise of describing "exotic" languages as though they were variants of Latin. In the seventeenth century Jesuit missionaries to the New World described a number of the aboriginal languages they found there in Latinate terms. They believed that their own knowledge of Latin provided them with all the information they needed to learn the new languages they came into contact with, and that the teaching materials they needed in their work should be based on a Latinate model. Many felt the languages were without rules and that they were doing the languages and their speakers a favor when they compiled grammars that used whatever rules they could find in Latin that might be useful. Others they made up on an *ad hoc* basis.

So far as English is concerned there is a tenth century grammar written by Aelfric in the belief that a mastery of Latin grammar would enable speakers of English to study the grammar of English. Aelfric's grammar is an English translation, somewhat rearranged, of Priscian's *Institutiones grammaticae*. Although it is designed to teach Latin, the grammar contains occasional comments from Aelfric on the English language. However, these grammatical observations are modeled on Latin. For example, Aelfric assumes that English has exactly the same eight parts of speech as Latin and that a knowledge of Latin is helpful in understanding and using English.

This high valuation of Latin was to continue. Sanford Meech's "Early Applications of Latin Grammar to English" shows how four early fifteenth-century manuscripts in English on the subject of Latin grammar provide "ample evidence . . . that borrowing of the concepts of Latin grammar was common in the fifteenth century, more than a hundred years before the earliest English grammars." Meech says that "the application of the concepts of Latin grammar to our language may have begun as a means of helping English schoolboys learn Latin." That was not the only consequence: it also helped shape how we have come to look at English.

In his influential *The Scholemaster* of 1570 Roger Ascham looked back to Latin, in this case Ciceronian Latin, for a linguistic model. Ascham believed that English had much to gain from emulating the high standards of Cicero's time and that English should fashion itself on Latin in as many ways as possible. This was a time when the English looked back to Latin, and to a lesser extent Greek, not only for grammatical terminology but also for terminology in subjects like mathematics, botany, medicine, and astronomy because of a feeling that English was inadequate. The early English grammars, therefore, tended to include all the characteristics of the grammars associated with the study of Latin: a Latinate grammar of English, rules for correct spelling and pronunciation, usage rules, etymologies, and long lists of rhetorical devices.

Some of the early grammars of English were written in Latin. William Lily's *A Shorte Introduction of Grammar* of 1567, often referred to as *Lily's Grammar*, became the standard grammar text of the English Renaissance. Except for a long introduction in English written by John Colet this grammar was written entirely in Latin and was based on the works of Donatus and Priscian. Shakespeare, Johnson, Milton, and Dryden used this grammar and it was the dominant school grammar for over two centuries. Other prominent grammars were Alexander Gil's *Logonomia Anglica* of 1619 and John Wallis's *Grammatica Linguae Anglicanae* of 1653. Many grammars written in English stressed the role of Latin, e.g., John Hewes's *A Perfect Survey of the English Tongue, taken according to the use and analogie of the Latine* of 1624, or commented on the inadequacies of English, e.g., H. Ward's *A Short, but Clear System of English Grammar, with exercises of bad English designed for the use of schools, and for those gentlemen and ladies who may want the assistance of a master* of 1777, or emphasized good speech, e.g., H. Groomridge's *The Rudiments of the English Tongue; or, a plain and easy introduction to English grammar: wherein the principles of the language are methodically digested. To which is added, an essay on elocution* of 1797.

We find an occasional admission that English was different from Latin, such as John Wallis's observation of 1674 – actually made in Latin – that too many grammars "bring our language too much to the Latin norm (because of which almost all who treat modern languages are in errror), and so introduce many useless principles concerning the cases, genders, and declensions of nouns, and the tenses, moods, and conjugations of verbs . . . and many other like things, which are all together alien to our language, and thus the confusion and obscurity they create are greater than the clarification they afford." No serious consideration was given to the implications of this observation. The usual conclusion was that English was ungrammatical and, if it differed from Latin, any such differences were not to its credit. We must remember that the purpose of these grammars was to teach their users enough about English so that they could turn their attention to the mastery of Latin. The grammars were not ends in themselves; they were merely the means to another – and, it was believed, greater – end, the learning of Latin.

Latin was a revered classical language in the eighteenth century and Roman civilization was much admired. Edward Gibbon could write of the second century as follows in his *The Decline and Fall of the Roman Empire*: "If a man were called to fix the period in the history of the world during which the condition of the human race was most happy and prosperous, he would, without hesitation, name that which elapsed from the death of Domitian to the accession of Commodus." Hovever, the new vernaculars could no longer be ignored. They had developed literatures, were associated with powerful states, and roused pride in those who used them. Much of that pride became focused on giving these vernaculars their own legitimacy, and it was widely believed that this legitimacy could best be expressed through giving them a classical dimension. The more a vernacular looked like Latin and had the trappings of Latin scholarship around it, the better it would be regarded in the world at large. A grammarian should try to resolve any grammatical problem by trying to see how Latin handled similar issues. This is how you turned a vernacular into a true language.

Since Latin was fixed in a written form, English would have to be fixed in a written form. There were Latin dictionaries so English would need a dictionary. That was Samuel Johnson's great achievement. English would also need a grammar which would show how it could be described as though it were Latin. Together, the dictionary and the grammar would define the language and give it the permanence and authority in the world that Latin had. It is not surprising then that in his "A Grammar of the English Tongue" that Johnson prefaced to his dictionary we find the English noun described as having the following cases: nominative, genitive, dative, accusative, vocative, and ablative. (It is also in this grammar that we find the first formulation of the *can–may* distinction so dear to the hearts of many purists.)

There were a few objectors in the eighteenth century to this approach but they did not get far with their protests. William Cobbett strongly rejected the use of Latinate terms for English, particularly for the verb system, which he correctly pointed out is completely different in the two languages. One of Cobbett's goals in writing *A Grammar of the English Language in a Series of Letters* was to attack the virtual monopoly that the classics held in the grammar schools and the notion that only those who knew Latin were capable of expressing themselves properly in English. Joseph Priestley in his

Rudiments of English Grammar of 1761 also completely eschewed the Latin model. Priestley pointed out that English does not have the whole Latin rigmarole of moods and tenses. In particular, it has no future tense and the use of *shall* and *will* with a following verb no more deserves a particular name (the future tense) than similar constructions of *do, have, can,* or *must* and a verb. He advocated trying to find out what the facts of English are, discovering how people actually use the language since "the custom of speaking is the original, and only just standard of any language," and avoiding any imposition of the writer's own view on what was found. However, Priestley was inconsistent in practice: while he strongly defended *It is me*, he could write in his own prose *It was we*, and he objected to expressions like *told my lord and I* and *my father and him have been*, which his contemporaries appear to have used quite readily, e.g., Lord Chesterfield, who wrote *You and me shall not be well together*. Cobbett and Priestley were almost alone in taking such positions. The great weight of Latin tended to smother all dissent.

Events elsewhere followed much the same course. For example, the writing of French grammars was also largely an exercise in translation from Latin and finding the nearest French equivalents. Some alternative proposals were made from time to time. For example, the Port-Royal grammarians Antoine Arnauld and Claude Lancelot tried in their *Grammaire générale et raisonnée* of 1660 to outline the principles of logic and reason that all languages exhibited – but French especially! Leopold Bouchot in 1760 in *Différence entre la grammaire et la grammaire générale raisonnée* argued to the contrary, that grammar and logic were unrelated. In *Traité de la formation mécanique des langues et des principes de l'étymologie* of 1765 Charles de Brosses argued for the importance of looking at the historical development of languages. Such views made little impression on either their contemporaries or those who followed and the Latinate tradition prevailed.

4 To Express Ourselves with Propriety

The two most influential grammars of English written in the eighteenth century were those of Robert Lowth and Lindley Murray.

Even today many teachers would feel quite comfortable with them. Lowth's grammar was used on both sides of the Atlantic but its greatest influence was in the United Kingdom; Murray's grammar was popular in the United States, where it became a standard school text selling over two million copies in the first half of the nineteenth century.

In his prefatory remarks to *A Short Introduction to Grammar* of 1762, Lowth, who became Bishop of London in his later years, asks whether or not it is correct that "the English language as it is spoken by the politest part of the nation, and as it stands in the writings of our most approved authors, oftentimes offends against every part of grammar." He answers that it does so offend, but adds that this does not mean that the language is "irregular and capricious." It has a grammar, and Lowth goes on in the main part of a brief work of 186 pages to describe English in Latinate terms.

In his opening remarks Lowth castigates "our best Authors" for their "mistakes" and "palpable errors in point of Grammar." He says: "The principal design of a Grammar of any Language is to teach us to express ourselves with propriety in that Language, and to be able to judge of every phrase and form of construction, whether it be right or not. The plain way of doing this is to lay down rules, and to illustrate them by examples." He intends to show what is right by showing what is wrong. His ultimate goal is to teach English grammar in such a way that students "would have some notion of what they were going about, when they should enter into the Latin Grammar."

Lowth has the usual parts of speech, nine in his case because he includes the article as a separate part. A "SUBSTANTIVE, or NOUN," is "the name of any thing conceived to subsist, or of which we have any notion." A verb is a "word by way of eminence, signifying to be, to do, or to suffer," a definition which thoroughly puzzled William Cobbett, who wondered what therefore were words like *toothache, fever, ague, rheumatism,* and *gout.* Surely verbs by such a definition!

Much of Lowth's work is given over to describing these nine parts of speech and we find the following sentence parsed for us: *The power of speech is a faculty peculiar to man, and was bestowed on him by his beneficent Creator for the greatest and most excellent uses; but alas! how often do we pervert it to the worst of purposes?* This sentence is typical of Lowth because a grammar must instruct not only in matters to do with language but also in matters to do with moral behavior.

Lowth prescribes what should be in English rather than describes what is. In doing so, he was merely conforming to the spirit of his day. Lowth does acknowledge the existence of variety in the language, listing, for example, both *rang* and *rung, sang* and *sung, sank* and *sunk,* and *swam* and *swum* as the past tenses of *ring, sing, sink,* and *swim* respectively. He also favors *his self* and *their selves* over *himself* and *themselves.* However, it is as a prescriptivist that we know Lowth today, as a rigid layer down of rules to be broken at peril, although he himself was a retiring individual who sought neither public recognition nor the mantle of authority.

We owe statements like the following to Lowth: "A sentence is an assemblage of words, expressed in proper form, and ranged in proper order, and concurring to make a complete sense." This is the kind of definition that generations of students have learned by heart since Lowth's time. However, it tells us nothing useful about English sentences. Without knowing what "an assemblage" is and what "proper form" and "proper order" are, we cannot create a single English sentence. These are the very stuff of grammar. Without them there can be no "complete sense." But nowhere are we told what these essential characteristics of English are.

Lowth has the following to say about using a preposition at the end of a clause or a sentence: "This is an Idiom which our language is strongly inclined to; it prevails in common conversation, and suits very well with the familiar style in writing; but the placing of the Preposition before the Relative is more graceful, as well as more perspicuous; and agrees much better with the solemn and elevated Style." "Elevated Style," "gracefulness," and "perspicuity," whatever they are, are to triumph over what the "language is strongly inclined to," with that *to* itself being a clause-ending preposition. Must we therefore conclude that Lowth chose not to write his grammar in an "elevated Style"? And if not, why not? (John Dryden also concerned himself with clause-ending prepositions and rewrote some of his prose to eliminate any instances of them.)

Lindley Murray's *English Grammar, Adapted to the Different Classes of Learners* was published in York in 1795 and in Boston in 1800. For Murray "English grammar [is] the art of speaking and writing English with propriety." Like Lowth before him, Murray believed that a grammar should point out both incorrect and correct usages. Consequently, his grammar is full of examples of the kind of English that he condemns. This pedagogical technique highlights those matters that are perceived to be errors. There is reason to believe that it lends authority to these errors, students not always remembering whether something is included in the grammar because it should be used or because it should be avoided. To those who do not make a particular "error" it points out a possible source of error, one that they may then proceed to introduce into their language.

We owe to Murray the popularization of that famous statement about the ungrammaticality of double negatives now included in most grammar books: "Two negatives, in English, destroy one another, or are equivalent to an affirmative." For countless millions they did not do so in Murray's day, had not done so before Murray's time, have not done since, nor will do in the future. The rule is one of logic not of language. However, it is a rule that has not been without influence on the users of English so that it is now observed by those who use standard English to the extent that it has become one of the hallmarks of that variety of English. (On the other hand, Murray did, approve of *none* followed by *are*.)

Murray was a pious man who found it impossible to keep his piety out of his grammar, but, like many such people, he was often more concerned with evil than with good and was keen to describe the very sins he condemned, e.g., all those disapproved uses that fill his grammar. Among these descriptions he interposed moral and religious statements to serve as examples, e.g., *Vice produces misery.* Consequently, Murray's grammar was like Lowth's before it, a grammar of rules and prohibitions, of examples of the good alongside examples of the bad, and of essentially Latinate statements about English mixed with appeals to grace, logic, and morality.

5 A Federal Language but a Latin Grammar

Noah Webster wanted to give Americans their own language, a "federal language," which would be a cohesive force in the new nation. He did provide them with their own dictionary but he thought they needed a grammar too. Such a grammar would "show . . . what a language *is*, not what it *ought to be*" he declared, but, in practice, he was a lot less liberal. His goal was to demonstrate that American English was every bit as worthy as British English and he wanted to show how it could be further improved.

Webster was from New England where people cultivated good manners and behavior. Etiquette books flourished, as did local ordinances against profanity and gossip. Loose language was condemned and much was made of "right behavior." This tradition continues today, finding expression in Emily Post-like columns in the press and the profusion of "social advice" books in bookstores. The tradition was not confined solely to New England: across the water Lord Chesterfield's famous letters of advice to his son are firmly rooted in the same tradition. This "moral" view of life was a particularly strong feature of existence in nineteenth-century New England and strongly influenced Webster.

Webster did not like Lowth's grammar, believing it to be filled with poorly translated ideas from Latin misapplied to English. He considered it a "stupid opinion" that "the only way of acquiring a grammatical knowledge of the English Tongue is first to learn a Latin Grammar." He maintained that: "In no field of study has progress been so slow as in the teaching of English grammar." Webster therefore published his own *A Grammatical Institute of the English Language* in three parts between 1783 and 1785, the second part of which, published in 1784, was a *A Plain comprehensive Grammar*. This grammar was to go through numerous editions until it was eventually overtaken by Murray's grammar.

We find some of Webster's views about grammar in his *Dissertations on the English Language* of 1789. For example, he preferred *Will I?* to *Shall I?* as the normal question form and declared *I have wrote* and *I have drove* to be "shocking improprieties." While he could advocate democracy in political matters, he rejected the same principle in language matters; no counting heads there for him. Like others, he feared the corruption of the language, sought authority, and was willing to appoint himself an arbiter of linguistic taste. Consequently, in his *Dissertations* Webster rejected *news* as a singular noun; no *What is the news?* for him. He declared of *Whom did you speak to?* that it "was never used in speaking, as I can find, and if so, is hardly English at all." He also preferred *Who did you speak to?* although he does not appear to have been particularly enthusiastic about it.

In his 1807 grammar, *A Philosophical and Practical Grammar of the English Language*, Webster was more accepting of the double negative, pointing out how frequently it was used, that it had a long history in the language, and that it was probably ineradicable. He did, however, reject the group genitive, i.e., expressions like *the King of Great Britain's soldiers*, because he could not find a Latin rule to account for it. He realized that pronouns "are often used in the place of sentences and adjectives, as well as of nouns," a good observation, and he proposed calling them *substitutes* instead. He was also aware that the use of *you was* was widespread and endorsed it, and he used *learn* in the sense of *teach*, as in "learn our children the letters of the alphabet."

A serious problem with Webster's grammars was that they often baffled those who tried to use them. While not approving of what Lowth had done, Webster could not free himself from the tradition in which Lowth's grammar took its origin. He necessarily had to work in that same tradition and when he moved any distance from it, as he did on occasion, he lost what followers he had. When Murray's grammar came along, it quickly replaced Webster's efforts. It was fully in the tradition and was clear in its prohibitions. The "standards" it upheld were unequivocal. Webster's dictionary and spelling books continued to be influential but his grammar was superseded.

6 The Legacy

The kind of grammar associated with Lowth and Murray dominated the teaching of the English language throughout the nineteenth century, retained considerable influence well into the twentieth, and lies behind much such teaching today where it occurs. Whereas at the beginning of the eighteenth century a variety of views could exist on language matters, in the nineteenth century uniformity of view took over. Those who considered the matter at all believed that the facts of English grammar had been decided in one way or another by their predecessors. All that was left for them to do was teach those facts. In the United States there was a strong emphasis on parsing, memorizing definitions, and "correcting" sentences. The teaching of grammar became a highly prescriptive matter, much like the teaching of religious doctrine. A grammar book was not unlike a catechism: a set of beliefs and facts to be learned, recited, tested, and followed, one that would lead you to a better life somewhere.

We can look briefly at just one grammatical point to show some of the consequences. By the nineteenth century grammar books were united in saying that the English "future tense" – it is not really a tense in the Latin sense because English requires a combination of verbs not a single inflected verb – requires the use of *shall* in the first person *(I, we shall go)* but *will* in the second and third persons *(you, he, she, it, they will go)*. To use *will* in the place of *shall* and *shall* in the place of *will* is to add a further element of determination about behavior in the future. This rule seems to have been first proposed in John Wallis's grammar of 1653 and then picked up by others. It may describe use in one or two varieties of English and it may also prescribe use among those who have adopted the rule because they believe it is important to follow prescriptive rules, epecially in writing. In actual speech there is considerable reduction of verbs like *shall* and *will*, as in *I'll go*, so it may be difficult to decide which modal verb is being used. The grammar-book distinction clearly does not describe practice for millions today. It did not for General Douglas MacArthur, who, on leaving the Philippines on March 12, 1942, declared "I shall return" when "good grammar" requires "I will return," and it obviously confused the reporter who wrote: "The future of the Planned Cultural Centre . . . shall be determined at a forthcoming meeting of the General Policy Committee" in what was a straight news report in a student newspaper. We must question Philip

Howard's assertion in *The State of the Language* that: "The nice but complex distinction between 'shall' and 'will' is dying; let it die," but not for Howard's reason: for most users of English the distinction has never existed!

The study of grammar has also developed a close association with the achievement of a sense of rectitude. Samuel Kirkham, a very influential nineteenth century grammarian, believed that the study of grammar not only benefited students in their use of language but also produced additional spiritual benefits. He went so far as to declare in *English Grammar, in Familiar Lectures* of 1829 that without such study a person could not "think, speak, read, or write with accuracy." He believed in the value of parsing, and of learning rules and definitions, and in the validity of the Latinate model for English. Kirkham's pedagogy relied heavily on correcting "incorrect" sentences, which he either took from writers or composed for the occasion. He regarded all the following sentences as incorrect: *Who did you walk with?*, *After I visited Europe, I returned to America*, *He would not believe that honesty was the best policy*, and *Five and eight makes thirteen*. He also disapproved of contractions such as *weren't, isn't,* and *hasn't*.

Kirkham was typical of his time. His great rival Goold Brown was of similar stamp. In his idiosyncratic, pedantic, and densely-crowded 1100-page *The Grammar of English Grammars* of 1851, Brown devoted much of his effort to parsing, correcting, and hunting out "errors": "ENGLISH GRAMMAR . . . is the art of reading, writing, and speaking the English language correctly." In his earlier *The Institutes of English Grammar* of 1823 Brown rejects each of the following as ungrammatical: *Who broke this slate? Me; I have never been asked this question; Who do you suppose it to be?; I shall walk out in the afternoon, unless it rains;* and *Men who are avaricious, never have enough*. Brown informs his readers that the "correct" forms are respectively *I, This question has never been asked me, Whom, rain,* and *that*. Brown's works are filled with instances of "bad" English. He advocates the memorization of rules and definitions, insists that writing should be used as a guide in speaking, and fills his work with moral injunctions. Like Kirkham, Brown makes no attempt to distinguish between the written language and the spoken language and assumes that his rules apply equally to both.

Nor does he make any attempt to relate any sentence or locution to a particular context; all are described as if they are used in a vacuum.

Lists of mistakes to be avoided are commonplace in Kirkham, Brown, and others. If one thing is right, then all others must be wrong. Grammatical issues are always discussed in this simple either-or dichotomy. Here, for example, is William Woodbridge on just that subject in *A Plain and Concise Grammar of the English Language; containing large exercises of parsing and in correct English* of 1800: "The only method of becoming correct in language is *carefully to observe* our mistakes . . . . Everyone who wishes to speak or write his language correctly, *must parse* that language – and carefully correct a variety of exercises of incorrect grammar, under all the rules of syntax. He must not only know it is wrong; but know the reason why."

In this approach to grammar the grammarian acts as a high priest who controls a sacred text. The teaching of grammar becomes an exercise in learning the dogma that the text contains. If what the text says about the real world differs from what we observe to occur there, so much the worse for the real world. Grammatical salvation lies in following the text and we must not be led astray by the practices of those around us. We must learn to follow the "good" and reject the "bad" and be prepared to expend the considerable effort that will be called for in doing this. And so on and so on. This has been called the doctrine of original sin in language teaching. In the late nineteenth and early twentieth centuries there was a strong reaction against such grammar teaching – it proved to be remarkably unsuccessful.

Even when linguists began to influence the statements that found their way into grammar books they found it difficult at first to free themselves entirely from this tradition. The *Essentials of English Grammar* of 1877 by William Dwight Whitney, Professor of Philology at Yale, was the first serious effort to provide American schools with a grammar that incorporated principles from the scientific study of language. Whitney tried to describe what English was like using the kind of scientific knowledge that was available to him. He pointed out that the concepts of "good usage" and "bad usage" were really social in nature. He defined "good English" as "those words and those meanings of them and those ways of putting them together, which are used by the best speakers, the people of best education"; what they did not approve of, Whitney called "bad English." Whitney could not escape prescriptivism in some of his statements. For example, he insisted on the *shall–will* distinction, called *It's me* "a popular inaccuracy," and "regretted" the fact that the subjunctive had almost entirely disappeared from English. None of these is a genuinely scientific observation; each is the kind of judgment we have come to expect within the tradition of grammatical study that we have inherited from the past

7 Understanding Language

The language tradition just described is still very influential. Almost everyone who has studied English grammar will tell you that there are eight parts of speech in the language. Various kinds of criteria go into defining these, but they are inconsistent with one another. Sentences are discussed in terms of "making sense." Rhetorical principles are used to classify both types of clause and types of sentence. There is also only one "right" answer to any controversial linguistic issue. Logic is constantly appealed to. The formal written language is assumed to set clear standards for the spoken language, even to the extent of guiding us in the pronunciation of words. There are authorities we can consult and linguistic police officers to tell us what to do and to issue tickets for violations.

We should not be surprised therefore that many people react the way they do to all of this. They claim not to "know" their grammar and they may actually apologize for "breaking the rules." Or they deny that there are any rules to be broken and assert that "English does not have a grammar." Or, as a result of what they have been taught about English, they feel insecure about using the language. They do not know why some things are "right" and others are "wrong," and they do not understand the relevance of their study of language to anything in their lives because they were not required to learn Latin. In the twentieth century many schools seeing the futility of efforts to teach grammar have stopped almost all such teaching. It is hard to see just what, if anything, has been lost as a result of neglect of this kind of grammatical study.

It would be much more rewarding to teach about grammar and rules in some other way. Language is a unique human characteristic. Those of us who speak English share a grammar of English. What is it like? Once we ask that question we can start looking at a whole cluster of issues.

We can look at how the language differs between speech and writing in order to try to find out why it differs. We might try to find out something about the spoken language, about the sounds we use and how we make them. Such a study might include some concern for how we use stress, pitch, and intonation in the language. It would certainly include becoming aware of how the spoken and written varieties of the language relate to each other, e.g., the relationships between sounds and letters and between pitch and intonation and punctuation, and of how they are also different from each other, e.g., an acknowledgment that the traditional "sentence" belongs to writing and that, in speaking, we often do not speak "in complete sentences" and that it is quite normal to "slur our words together." We could also look at the different varieties of the spoken language.

It might be useful to see what types of words we have in the language. We may still want to talk about nouns, verbs, adjectives, conjunctions, and so on, but how do we know something is a noun or a verb or an adjective or a conjunction? *Stone* is a noun because, among other things, we can have *a stone* and *two stones*. *Old* is an adjective because we also have *older* and *oldest*. (We cannot have *an old* and *two olds* nor *stoner* and *stonest*.) *Wall* is another noun. We can have *an old wall*, *a stone wall*, and also *an old stone wall* but not *a stone old wall*. *Old* and *stone* can both modify wall, i.e., both adjectives and nouns can modify nouns, but when both an adjective and a noun together modify another noun the adjective modifier must precede the noun modifier, so giving us *an old stone wall* and making *a stone old wall* ungrammatical. Such an approach can easily be extended. It will also show us that we have some very special words in the language, words like *the*, *a*,

127

very, rather, can, may, do, not, that, to (as in *to sing* where it is definitely not a preposition), and *whether,* to name but a few, whose uses we cannot ignore in the language and simply avoid discussing when we content ourselves with assigning arbitrary parts-of-speech labels to them.

We can look at the way we build up phrases and clauses and how we combine these. For example, English verb phrases like *should have been told* and *might be going* are very different in their structures from single, inflected, Latin verbs, and, while English has many ways of talking about time, it has only two clearly marked grammatical tenses, a "present tense," e.g., *I go,* and a "past tense," e.g., *I went.* We also do talk about future possibilities: *I'll go, I go tomorrow, I am about to go, I'm going to go,* and so on, but there is no grammatical marking which exclusively indicates "future tense" in English.

It will be of interest to find out how the various forms of the verb *do* are functioning in the following sentences: *Do you want it?, He doesn't know,* and *He does like her.* They are certainly functioning differently from the *do* in *He is doing his homework.* It will also be of interest to try to find out why in a sentence like *John expects to go,* we know that *John* is the subject of both *expects* and *go* (John will go) but in *John expects him to go* we know that some other male than John will go (He, not John, will go). Moreover, in *He expects him to go* we know that the *he* and the *him* must refer to two different people. There is a clear grammatical principle here; just exactly what is it? Both *John took Sally out last night* and *John took the garbage out last night* are good English sentences, but *John took Sally and the garbage out last night* suggests a bizarre set of circumstances. Why so? Once again there is an interesting point of grammar here, just as there is in considering two sentences like *Joan wants someone to hold* and *Joan wants someone to hold her* with respect to how we know who is to do the holding and who is to be held.

There are many such grammatical issues in the language most of which traditional grammar books either ignore or find uninteresting. However, they are essential grammatical aspects of English, aspects which are quite different from Latin. Discussing them also requires at times the use of terms that differ considerably from those we use to describe Latin. As soon as we take such matters seriously, we find ourselves confronted with the enormous complexity of the language. Far from not having a grammar, English, like every other language we know, has a grammar that no-one has yet succeeded in describing fully. Perhaps the best attempt we have had so far is a grammar entitled *A Comprehensive Grammar of the English Language*, the work of Randolph Quirk, Sidney Greenbaum, Geoffrey Leech, and Jan Svartvik. This grammar is 1779 pages long; its authors do not claim that it is a "complete" grammar of English but only that it is "comprehensive."

We might try to deal sensibly with the variations in usage that we meet. Rather than condemn certain usages out of hand, we might learn something about the language by looking at usages that differ from those we are sometimes encouraged to prefer. Why do some people say the following: *He's the baddest boy in the class, You was going, They likes to do it, He's silly is Billy, Give it me, Is it yourn?, Me and him will go, I want for him to do it, It'll do thee good, He done her wrong, We might could do it,* and *I dinna care?* Surely it makes more sense to try to find out why people vary in their choices between *It's me* and *It's I* and *To whom did you send it?* and *Who did you send it to?*, and over such matters as the use of *like* as a conjunction , *different to, from,* or *than*, double negatives, *If I was, everyone* followed by *their*, and so on, than simply to impose some arbitrary rule!

None of this would threaten or destroy the language. In every other serious discipline the practitioners respect their data. Only in language study do many of those who seek to influence others turn their backs on data in favor of opinion. But then that too is something we will have to learn to understand if we are ever to effect any meaningful change in attitudes toward language.

CHAPTER SIX

Some Consequences
of Literacy

Many of us associate language with writing to the extent that we cannot separate the two. As Leonard Bloomfield wrote in an article entitled "Literate and Illiterate Speech" in 1927, "almost anyone except a professed student of language explains matters of speech by statements which really apply only to writing." Writing often appears to be much more important that speaking because it has a permanence that speaking lacks. Learning to write also cost some of us dearly: we can remember painful hours spent learning to spell, trying to express ourselves on paper, writing assignments and tests, and being judged for our all too frequent failures. But who can remember learning to speak? That came so easily and required no effort at all. Something won at great cost is likely to be more highly valued than something gained so easily.

We must remember, however, that writing is a fairly recent human invention. People got along in the world for many tens of thousands of years before they made any attempt to represent what they said in a permanent form. The alphabetic system that we use today for English also evolved out of other systems; now alphabetic writing systems predominate in the world.

Today, we assume that literacy is a "good thing," i.e., that everyone should know how to read and write. It was not always so. Nor is it easy to say what exactly we mean by literacy or illiteracy. As Carlo Cipolla explains in *Literacy and Development in the West*, "any given degree of illiteracy has quite a different meaning when related to different societies such as Europe in the ninth century and Europe one thousand years after." Some people go so far as to say that literacy, especially alphabetic literacy, has transformed our cultural possibilities. We may not agree with them, but we cannot deny that it has changed our views of language. Much of what we believe about language and seek to do with language derives from how we have approached the written word in the past. Without that tradition we would almost certainly have very different views of language.

1 The Beginnings of our Literate Tradition

The earliest writings that we have are from Mesopotamia. They suggest that writing first developed as an aid to memory: certain records were committed to writing. The evidence is not conclusive nor do we know how long it took for people to exploit their new invention. However, in general, new inventions are first put to old uses and only later develop new uses, and there is little reason to assume that writing was treated any differently. The first written documents served as records: they acted as inventories or confirmed oral agreements. One particularly interesting inventory in English history, though written in Latin, is the *Domesday Book* of 1086 in which William the Conqueror, who may have been illiterate himself, had a list made of the contents of his newly acquired England.

We know that in places like ancient Egypt, ancient Babylon, and ancient China only very few people used writing. It soon became associated with religion, power, and exclusivity. From the beginnings writing proved to be a conservative force in the societies that used this new invention.

In ancient Greece writing seems to have served only the purposes of business and trade when it was first introduced about 800 BCE. Its uses were then extended into other areas of life. Eventually, in places like Athens there was widespread literacy among males so that it was an insult to say of an Athenian either that he could not read or that he could not swim. We must remember that Athenian culture was an oral one which prized argumentation and rhetoric. In *Phaedrus* Plato makes Socrates, who does not appear ever to have written anything himself, condemn writing because writing corrupts memory, allows people to forget, and forces them to rely on something external. There was not a great deal to read in Athens for books were few and precious. The Spartans were less enthusiastic about the written word than the Athenians but the upper classes of Sparta were literate; however, they preferred deeds to words and, when they spoke, they preferred plain speaking to the rhetorical embellishments of the Athenians.

Considerable and widespread literacy existed in ancient Rome and her possessions, as we can see from the graffiti of Pompeii. Boys learned to read through drill, repetition, and memorization, and the methods used encouraged discipline and achievement. Grammatical study was emphasized with its aim the reading of the great poets. The teacher explained difficult words and points to students, ensured that they understood the metrics, and insisted on correctness in reading aloud. The Romans also appreciated the importance of the alphabet. In *Institutio oratoria* Quintilian stressed the importance of learning the alphabet quickly and accurately as a prerequisite to the rest of his educational program. He believed that individual letters were the building blocks from which everything else in the language was constructed. You learned your alphabet first and then you learned your words.

More advanced education in Rome led to the systematic study of grammar and rhetoric, with its ultimate goal the production of articulate leaders. Since the Romans looked back to the Greeks and their culture, ideas, language, and literature, they introduced a classical, historical orientation into their thinking about culture, education, language, and writing. They favored rote learning, repetition, reading aloud, and recitation in a highly disciplined environment that would ensure students developed the right moral tone.

There were small libraries in Rome and a book industry of sorts, the Romans using slave labor to reproduce manuscripts in quantity. A bookseller like Atticus would have as many as 500 copies of a manuscript reproduced for sale. Books could exist because authorship found support. Authors like Horace and Pliny the Younger gave readings of their works both privately and publicly before turning them over to booksellers for more widespread distribution.

The literary language of Rome, the one that found its way into such manuscripts and which was taught to pupils, was from the very beginning a conservative and narrow variety of Latin. The Romans exported this same variety to their empire as the true language of Rome and it was different from the vulgar Latin used by the soldiers of the Roman armies and the merchants who followed these soldiers. When the Romans taught this language to foreigners, they insisted on a pronunciation that followed the written language, on students learning the grammar of that language, and on mastery of the rhetorical skills they prized.

By Virgil's time in the first century BCE, a considerable gap had opened up between the written and spoken varieties of Latin and we can get some idea of the full range of the language from reading the works of Plautus and Petronius, who deliberately introduced popular speech into their works. As this gap increased, so did the need for instructions in the classical, written variety of the language in order that Romans – and later others – could continue to read Cicero, Livy, Ovid, Lucretius, and Virgil. We often fail to realize that Roman civilization did not exist at a single point in time but covered many centuries. The Romans were aware of the changes in their language over that period; in the later years of empire they realized that the language they spoke was different from the language they read in their classics. They placed a much higher value on the written language than on the spoken language and, like many in the centuries since, regarded the widening gap between the two as a sign of deterioration.

In ancient Greece and Rome there had been a considerable amount of literacy of a secular nature and when the Roman Empire went into decline literacy went into a decline along with it. The Latin language did live on with its written form protected eventually by the Church, but in the various parts of the Roman Empire the different forms of vulgar Latin became the earliest forms of the emerging vernaculars. For hundreds of years literacy and learning almost vanished from sight. The great Emperor Charlemagne of the eighth century was almost certainly illiterate even though he was interested in promoting education and literacy. He could afford to be illiterate, because he could employ literates

133

to read and write for him, literacy having become a narrow, vocational skill. When King Alfred the Great of England tells us in 893 that there were many who knew how to read English in England, we must wonder how many he could have meant for it is likely that literacy and learning were not at all widespread at that time. There appears not to have been an educated public in Europe between the sixth and twelfth centuries; any learning that did exist was confined almost entirely to the Church.

Christianity continued its spread as the Roman Empire declined. Early Christianity was essentially a populist religion of the spoken word and of proselytizing in the vernacular: "He that hath ears, let him hear." It was anti-authoritarian and anti-elitist, and only later, when it became heavily institutionalized and ritualized in the Church of Rome, did it become – like Judaism before it and Islam after – a "religion of the book." At that time it also became heavily Latinized. The Church used literacy for its own purposes: to be *litteratus*, "literate," meant to be schooled in Latin and in theology.

Western medieval education and literacy were designed to serve the goals of a monopolistic Church in which Latin played a central role as a lingua franca. By the seventh century the seven liberal arts had been established as the curriculum in education. These arts consisted of the indispensable (so far as training clergy was concerned) trivium of grammar, logic, and rhetoric, and the quadrivium of music, arithmetic, geometry, and astronomy. The language of this education was Latin and instruction in Latin involved learning how to read and write the language correctly and achieving familiarity with its literary classics. This Latin was a "dead," written Latin and the contact with such a variety of a language profoundly influenced all thinking about language. The general goal was education within a Christian framework, but, to accomplish this goal, a Christian theology had to be united with parts of a Graeco-Roman pagan tradition to form a new tradition.

The system was one in which all education was in a dead, foreign language. There was almost no vernacular education. The language that was prized was Latin. It was to be learned through a system of teaching which, acutely short of books, called for considerable memorization, the catechismatic elicitation of responses, and a close reading of a limited range of material. One of the most famous books used in medieval education was the *Doctrinale* of Alexander of Villedieu of 1199, which was based largely on Priscian's work. Written in hexameters, it was extremely popular for about three centuries throughout western Europe.

The overall purpose of a medieval education was not to seek to improve this life but to secure an after life. The authority for such practices was a Church that proclaimed a vision of truth and certainty. Preoccupied with the eternal and immutable, the Church turned its back on the natural world. Students were supposed to learn the truth about plants, stars, and other natural phenomena from consulting the writings of old authorities rather than by looking around them, for example, by reading what Aristotle and Pliny had to say about how many teeth a horse has rather than by looking into a horse's mouth.

Some did become literate outside this tradition. We have records of poems, riddles, chronicles, etc., in the vernaculars of the time. We know that in many cases these existed mainly as aids to memory, for example a twelfth century charter addressed to "all who shall hear and see this charter." We also know that there was a popular distrust of written records because there is evidence that as late as the twelfth century oral testimony was preferred over written documentation.

Even though William of Normandy had conquered England in 1066 and brought Norman French with him, by the thirteenth century literacy was thoroughly associated with being learned in Latin and with being in some kind of holy orders, being *clericus* or a clerk, as is Chaucer's clerk in "The Clerk's Tale" in *The Canterbury Tales*. It was possible to claim "benefit of clergy" and escape harsh punishment, even death, for committing a crime by being able to read a verse or two of Latin from the Bible. Eventually, so much use was made of this benefit that in the sixteenth it was restricted to lesser crimes (but also extended to women). However, the benefit of clergy was not removed from English law – and then not completely – until 1706.

If in 1300 in England literacy meant literacy in Latin, the language of learning, nevertheless French and English were also widely used and there was some literacy in both. It was not until

English won its own struggle against French that literacy in English could become an important issue. It could not become so until good reasons existed for people to want to read and write in English. There had to be uses for English literacy. Literacy in a language is always possible but without good reasons improbable.

2 The Printed Word

In fifteenth-century Europe Latin had become moribund as a spoken language but remained well established as the language of education. The vernaculars had not fully established themselves; they had none of the prestige of Latin and appeared disordered to their users. It was into such a world that printing was introduced.

Printing was one of several changes that occurred in the West at this time. The new vernaculars were in widespread use, there was a growing interest in education accompanied by an increase in literacy, and people were congragating in towns and cities. Society itself was ready for change, but the advent of printing did not by itself bring about that change. It may even have given a temporary boost to old ways, to Latin and its authority, because the first printed materials gave wider disssemination than before to very traditional materials.

Printing, which itself depended on the abilty to produce paper in large quantities, a much earlier Chinese innovation, was introduced into Europe by Johann Gutenberg and into England by William Caxton, when he established his press in Westminster in 1476. Like other printers, Caxton had to make choices both in what to print and how to print it. Such choices made at the beginning of an innovation as important as printing often have a profound effect on what follows. Caxton was fully aware of the difficulties involved in printing in the vernacular, for example of the variation that existed in the language and of its image as being "rude," in contrast to French. Caxton chose to print materials in the literary dialect of English with which he was familiar, using the spelling conventions of that variety, although not always with consistency. Printing, therefore, quickly established one variety of English as being more important than others as printers followed Caxton's example.

In England, as in the rest of western Europe, printing did more than favor one variety of a language. It gave the language itself a boost just when it was most needed by allowing vernacular materials to be printed in large quantities for an audience ready for such materials. This development ended any hope there might have been of making Latin a universal language. The availability of materials in English encouraged the development of popular literacy. The earliest printed materials were just like those that had existed in the manuscripts that had to be reproduced so laboriously before the advent of printing. The earliest books even looked like manuscripts. There was an immediate, enormous increase in the availabilty of religious texts, sermons, tracts, technical manuals, and books on magic and the occult.

Printing allowed the growing demand for books to be met and then created a further demand, mainly among middle-class readers. Suddenly print brought learning to readers; they did not have to go in search of it, as did the wandering scholars of the medieval period. A market was also created for instructional materials related to reading, for books such as ABCs, the forerunners of the later hornbooks and primers. An ABC generally contained the alphabet together with the Lord's Prayer and other simple religious matters. An early one, for example, licensed in the late 1550s, is entitled *An abc for children in englysshe with syllables.*

The advent of print created problems for the Church, which tended to resist translating the Bible into the vernacular languages and printing any translations in large quantities. In 1546 the Council of Trent attempted to prohibit such vernacularization. One reason for this opposition was the belief that translations would further reduce the number of those who knew Latin; another was that in translation the Bible would lose some of its mystery to the faithful; still another was a fear that the Bible would be mistranslated; and, finally, the vernaculars were thought to be inappropriate for something so important. As early as the eleventh century, in a letter to the King of Bohemia, Pope Gregory VII quite explicitly rejected the idea of translating the Bible into a vernacular, declaring that it would lose its esteem and be misunderstood. However, the most important reason for such resistance was that the Church was reluctant to surrender its monopolistic practices.

In fourteenth- and fifteenth-century England people like John Wycliffe and the Lollards insisted on translating the Bible into English. Like others elsewhere in Europe, they believed that the common people should be allowed to read the Bible in their own vernaculars so that they could discover its truths directly and interpret its message for themselves. The Church treated them as heretics for their efforts and states regarded them as subversives. Official moves were made to prevent translations by banning and licensing but the movement toward vernacular bibles could not be stopped, in England at least. Later, it was actually encouraged there by the sixteenth-century break with the Church of Rome and eventually found its fullest expression in the King James Bible of 1611, the climactic work in a sequence of official vernacular Bibles in English.

The Bible was not the only book the printers produced. As the demand for printed material grew so did the range of materials printed. We must not forget that from the very beginning of printing what emerged from the new presses was a mixture of the sacred and profane, of the scientific and the non-scientific, of the sound and the spurious. Much like today in fact! All such materials whatever their nature immediately acquired a certain authority merely by being in print. Again, like today, as we see from comments we hear people make like *I read it in a book, The paper said this morning that . . .*, or *The dictionary says . . . .* Printing has that effect on many people: it tends to give an aura of "truth" and "authority" not only to anything that is written but also to how it is written.

The mass production of printed materials eventually brought about standardization of everything from spelling on the one hand to content on the other. It also brought about a different kind of "memory" to those who became literate, the memory of written records. It made such records and their storage and retrieval important, and it brought us the possibility of comparing written records. It allowed for new forms of expression in language. Above all, it brought with it a heavy weight of authority to the variety of language in which all these materials were created, in our case a standardized, written English, but a standardized, written English regarded as though it were some kind of neo-Latin.

3 Spelling Words Correctly

One of the lasting effects of the development of printing has been the system of spelling we now have. That system evolved very slowly. Old English was written in an alphabet that fairly closely resembles the one we use today but it took almost a millennium to arrive at the 26 letters we use today and the system of punctuation that we associate with these. The writing system of Old English did contain some relics of an older, Runic alphabet but these diasappeared under later French scribal tradition. There is one relic of the older alphabet still extant, the *Ye* in deliberate archaic use in phrases like *Ye olde tea shoppe* with this *Y* being the modern reflex of an old Runic letter pronounced *th*. *Ye* is really no more than another way of writing *the*.

French scribes later modified the spelling practices they had inherited from Old English. The vocabulary of English was expanded by heavy borrowing from French, Latin, and Greek along with borrowing of some of their spelling conventions. Later, it would be further modified as English borrowed words – and often their accompanying exotic spellings – from almost everywhere in the world. By the mid-fifteenth century the clerks in Chancery in Westminster had developed a spelling system for English that closely resembles the one we have today, but it did not have much use outside official documents. Nor did those outside Chancery who wrote the language feel any great need either to follow its example or to be consistent in spelling. When writing was a personal matter, spelling could also be a personal matter.

The introduction of printing in the final quarter of the fifteenth century changed such customs but not immediately. Printing spread so fast at first that it did not necessarily draw on the spelling tradition associated with Chancery as printers hurried to get new materials into the hands of readers. Each printing shop had its own practices. There was a considerable variety of spellings in the earliest printed materials and it was not until the period between 1550 and 1650 that people began to think that English spelling should be stabilized. Elizabethan books vary widely in their spelling and Shakespeare is but one of the spellings we find for the playwright's name. By 1700 the stabilization of spelling had been achieved and people became conscious for the first time of the need to "spell correctly."

However, it was not at all easy to spell correctly by this time. Not only had English spelling been influenced by a French scribal tradition and the vocabulary absorbed many words from other languages, often in their original spellings, but English had undergone some important sound changes. One of these, the Great Vowel Shift of the fifteenth and sixteenth centuries, drastically changed the relationship of many vowel letters to the sounds they represented. In the sixteenth century too certain words were deliberately respelled for etymological reasons, e.g., *debt* and *scissors*. Consequently, many spellings were not easy one to learn. The written and spoken varieties of the language also differed in many respects and these differences caused considerable bewilderment. Moreover, the spoken language of the time was extremely varied whereas the written language was much more uniform. We should not be surprised, therefore, to find that in such circumstances those concerned with language issues tended to look to the written variety as a source of authority in deciding matters of pronunciation.

The English spelling system has always had its critics. Usually the letters themselves are not criticized although George Bernard Shaw thought we should start again with a completely new alphabet. Compared with the letter shapes of other alphabets, Cyrillic and Arabic for example, our letter shapes have certain advantages: a good mixture of ascenders and descenders, an avoidance of uniform block shapes and diacritical ornamentation, only two possible shapes for each letter, and simple joining conventions for writing by hand. The result is a legible look to anything written in our alphabet

Spelling reformers complain about the inconsistent way in which our alphabet represents the sounds of English. One of first attempts to reform spelling dates to the beginning of the thirteenth century when the monk Orm tried to introduce a systematic way of doubling vowel and consonant letters. The sixteenth century witnessed considerable controversy over English spelling. Thomas Smith, John Hart, Alexander Gil, and Charles Butler argued strongly in favor of reform. Hart, for example, in his *Orthographie* of 1569 wanted to abandon "custom" for "reason." Richard Mulcaster in *The First Part of the Elementarie* of 1582, however, argued against any such change, preferring instead that efforts should be directed toward stabilizing the spelling of English through "consent" rather than changing it abruptly.

The dictionaries of the eighteenth century not only stabilized spelling but also fixed it so rigidly that today there is little tolerance of any deviation. Being unable to spell correctly is regarded almost like sinning and being proud of it – it meets with strong condemnation! Spelling reform also continues to be a popular cause. Among the many spelling reformers we can name Benjamin Franklin, Noah Webster, George Bernard Shaw, Isaac Pitman, Andrew Carnegie, who helped to fund the Simplified Spelling Board, Theodore Roosevelt, Mark Twain, and Sir James Pitman, the deviser of the Initial Teaching Alphabet. Linguists too have been interested in spelling: Henry Sweet, James Murray of *OED* fame, Daniel Jones, Harold Orton, R. E. Zachrisson, and Axel Wijk.

English spelling continues to bedevil many of us. In November, 1992 the Manchester *Guardian* reported on a Gallup survey that asked a thousand adults to spell six words: *accommodation, business, height, necessary, separate,* and *sincerely. Height* proved to be the easiest of these words to spell but still trapped 16 percent, and only 27 percent spelled *accommodation* correctly. Overall, one-sixth of those sampled spelled all the words correctly but one-tenth got all of them wrong. With many finding spelling so difficult we constantly find new proposals for reform produced for our approval. However, these proposals are often completely misguided and show litle understanding of how letters and sounds relate to each other or of simple phonetic facts about the language. (They also often display completely erroneous ideas about the nature of language itself.) They are part of a long western tradition in which the relationship between letters and sounds has been misunderstood.

A similar lack of understanding can be found in many of the proponents of "phonics" as a way of teaching reading. Since the English writing system employs an alphabet, it is a "phonic" one, but phonics as a method of teaching the relationships of letters and sounds requires that those who use it have a good knowledge of these relationships. Large numbers of phonics practitioners, including many "experts," lack such knowledge. (A simple test: most varieties of English have 24 consonant sounds and just over a dozen contrastive vowels and diphthongs but how many phonics teachers know exactly what these are?)

Once we let ourselves get carried away by the power of the written word and its letters strange things happen. Some enthusiasts have gone so far as to believe that letters can be studied as fascinating objects in their own right, i.e., that they have certain mystical properties. The discovery of exotic scripts served only to increase this kind of interest. One idea was that letters had inherent sounds and that different writing systems reflected fundamental incompatibilities among languages. Another was that the actual shapes of the letters used in a particular language could tell us something about the basic characteristics of that language. They can tell us nothing at all about the language. Such misunderstandings arise from studying written languages, either dead or alive, and having no idea about the nature of language, phonetics, or the evolution of writing systems.

Most would-be reformers agree that we should be able to tell how to pronounce a word from the way in which we write that word. They have reversed the original connection between speech and writing. Writing began as a way of representing sounds in a permanent form; now most people believe that the representations of writing should tell us how to say something. We no longer try to find letters to represent sounds but worry about how to pronounce letters. In reality, we must do both depending on whether we are writing, i.e., finding letters for sounds, or reading, i.e., finding sounds for letters, but most of us, having forgotten the two-sidedness of this operation, now give an unwarranted primacy to the written form of the language.

4 Becoming Literate in English

The rise of the vernaculars and the invention of printing provided a great impetus to literacy and education. The vernaculars were used more and more for record-keeping, personal letters, and works of literature so that eventually Latin was abandoned for just about everything except religion and advanced education. People became literate first in the vernacular and only then in Latin. But it was literacy in Latin that continued to have the greater prestige.

Vernacular literacy helped to validate the vernaculars. It gave them the written forms they badly needed. But it also drew attention to what many perceived to be their shortcomings: their variety, their essential orality, and their "deficiencies" in comparison to Latin. One consequence was that they were treated like Latin, as fixed, written languages rather than as varied, spoken ones. Another was that, while they might be used in the beginning stages of education, they were used there primarily as a means to prepare students for the eventual study of Latin.

The Church and Latin were the two most important influences on education in medieval times. Later, as society grew more secular, the Church still retained considerable authority in educational matters and even as the vernaculars grew in strength Latin maintained its prestige. Instruction in reading and literacy, whether given in ABC, dame, song, parish, chantry, town, monastery, guild, or grammar schools was religiously and morally inclined. Education in the West has never entirely abandoned its connection with either the teachings of a specific religion or morals. Nor has it shed that early connection with the teaching of Latin.

Some titles of early school books in English are very instructive in this regard. Fifteenth-century books of manners have titles like *The Book of Courtesy, The Book of Nurture, The Babees Book, A Little Report of How Young People Should Behave,* and *The School of Virtue and Book of Good Nurture for Children and Youth to Learn their Duty By.* Fifteenth-century primers have titles like *A Primer in English, with certain prayers and godly meditation very necessary for all people that understand not the Latin tongue, A Primer and a Catechism, and also the notable fairs in the Calendar,* and *The Primer and Catechism set forth with many godly prayers.*

The Elizabethan grammar schools were devoted to the teaching of Latin with English used as a bridge into Latin. These schools took boys at about the age of eight who already knew their ABCs, having learned these before arriving at the grammar schools, possibly in dame or ABC schools, known as petty schools. The grammar schools proceeded to educate them in Latin: they learned the parts of speech and the rules of syntax, read Latin literature, translated and paraphrased. A favorite text was Lily's *Grammar*, which gained royal apppproval. The grammar-school regime was harsh: it employed rote learning, double translation from Latin to English and then back to Latin again, and corporal punishment for failure of any kind.

Roger Ascham, who wrote *The Scholemaster* in English in 1570, stated the aim of such education: to "understand, write and speak the Latin tongue." However, Ascham also saw a place for English in the curriculum but only for English studied as though it were Latin. He believed that just as the Romans had modeled themselves on the best Greek authors, so the English should model themselves on the best Latin writers and thereby their language would achieve "eloquence." On the other hand, Richard Mulcaster placed a higher value on English and wanted vernacular education to precede rather than follow classical education. Edmund Coote's *The English Schoole-Maister* of 1596, which went through 54 editions with the last published as late as 1737, was concerned with various aspects of the teaching of English, such as ensuring that pupils learn acceptable spellings and pronunciations, write with grammatical correctness, and master the vocabulary that has come to us from the classical languages. However, Coote treated English in almost every way just like Latin.

In Tudor and Stuart times elementary education focused on teaching children to read rather than to write. These two activities were clearly separated; many children learned to read but never learned to write. We must remember that writing was not initially associated with reading but was regarded as a separate, independent, specialized skill. Those who did not go to grammar schools read nothing in school except ABCs, catechisms, primers, psalters, the Bible, and prayer books. Reading also meant reading aloud, often as part of a group, and it often involved learning by heart. (Private, silent reading is a modern innovation.) The skill of reading aloud became a prized skill, but one that encouraged a particular kind of enunciation, a reverence for the written word, and an undervaluation of comprehension of what was being read. Although there was a wide range of reading material available outside school, a strong oral culture persisted, one largely uninfluenced by written materials. The materials that did exist tended to reinforce rather than undermine that oral culture.

The Reformation produced a certain ambivalence toward literacy. Protestantism encouraged reading of the Bible, but at the same time did not encourage learning. Learning was associated with authority, particularly the Church of Rome, and the Reformation had been an attack on long-established authority. Consequently, the seventeenth century saw some hesitancy about the development of education. Was it wise to promote education in a period of political and social confusion? It was a century of struggle between orthodoxy and heresy in which either conformism or heresy could cost you your life depending on the historical moment. It was a time in which there was a ready supply of calendars, hagiographic lives of saints, romances, pamphlets, treatises, and manuals, but also of works regarded as blasphemous and seditious. It was not a time favorable to the spread of either education or literacy, and historians agree that little or no progress occurred in either area in seventeenth-century England.

In the eighteenth century, an era often referred to as the Enlightenment, a considerable emphasis was placed on education and literacy. The promotion of these was tied to social control, moral advancement, and serious nation-building. Above all, a stable social order was sought and a respect for authority demanded. The eighteenth century saw the development of dictionaries and grammars, a "fixing" of the language, the setting of standards, and further reinforcement of the idea that language was something written rather than something spoken.

Religious groups continued to be heavily involved in education on both sides of the Atlantic. For example, before the mid-nineteenth century the Protestant religion and its associated schools were the prime forces involved in raising literacy in colonial New England. However, this was literacy among males because females were left largely uneducated, at least in formal institutions. From the late seventeenth century on *The New England Primer*, a highly moralistic speller and reader, was the most popular first school book with some three million copies sold between 1690 and 1840. The Bible was another popular school book.

Not everyone everywhere thought that this spread of education was in the best interests of society. *The Rights of Man*, published by Thomas Paine in 1791, found a wide audience with well over a million copies in print at the time of Paine's death. *Observations on the Nature of Civil Liberty* of 1776 by Richard Price was also popular. Literacy was thought to have helped pave the way to such outbursts as the French Revolution. Governments feared such writings, which they saw as seditious, and the English government issued a Royal Proclamation in 1792 against "seditious writings" and instituted a series of political trials. In 1807 the President of the Royal Society argued against the extension of education to the laboring classes on the basis that it would "be prejudicial to their morals and happiness," lead to discontent, encourage insubordination and indolence, and enable them to read seditious pamphlets, vicious books, and publications against Christianity. Education and literacy not directed toward maintaining authority might succeed in undermining it.

The nineteenth century saw a great expansion of education but also witnessed the Industrial Revolution, which proved to be a mixed blessing for the laboring masses. The new industries consumed cheap labor, required minimal skills in the work force, and exploited all they could, including children. Before the reforms of 1830 the English government was deliberately non-interventionist, and afterwards concerned itself only reluctantly with the social consequences of what was happening, taking until 1870 to introduce an Education Act that provided a minimal education for all. In North America the situation was never as bad but the United States had problems of another kind, those of institutional racism, massive immigration, and westward expansion.

Nineteenth-century education in England was devoted to morality, restraint, and the preservation of the existing social system. It was designed to counteract perceived tendencies toward crime, poverty, and disorder. Increases in education and literacy would, reformers believed, decrease immorality, crime, and poverty, and ensure progress. That was the great nineteenth-century idea, one that still finds currency today. Children should be rescued from their parents' ways, from ignorance, sloth, bad linguistic habits, immorality, drunkenness, and vice. (In the late twentieth century we added sex, drugs and rock 'n' roll to this list!) Children should be taught to be moral, industrious, obedient, and literate.

To achieve such a condition, they would learn their ABCs, and they would do this through disciplined rote-learning in a system that ensured social deference. They would be introduced to the "correct" variety of the language and all other varieties would have scorn heaped on them. They would learn what they had to learn unquestioningly. They would be told what was right and what was wrong. Following the right and avoiding the wrong was the proper path to salvation. The next life was the important one, not this one. There need not, therefore, be any great connection between what went on in the schoolroom and what went on outside it. The schoolroom itself was also a rather harsh environment of few books, of slates to write on, of large numbers of pupils, and of poorly trained teachers whose main problem was often keeping some sort of order. The achievements of such schools were minimal, the majority of children learning to do little more than bark at print.

For the masses there was nothing that could be described as intellectual in the curriculum. In fact, there were two curricula, one for the masses and the other for the elite. For those at the very top, the males at least, there were the great public schools of England, which came into prominence in the nineteenth century with their emphasis on male-bonding, a caste-like social superiority, a rigid classical education, and harsh discipline. It was an education that, according to a famous apocryphal story, would allow Sir Charles Napier, the British commander in India, to inform the War office in London that he had captured Sind by sending the simple message *Peccavi* (I have sinned). At a lower level the grammar schools continued their tradition, although here, as the Taunton Commission of 1868 found, nearly half of the endowed grammar schools were no longer teaching any Latin or Greek.

In North America there was the same emphasis on order, discipline, and morality in education. The overriding concern was with assimilation, nation-building, and the achievement of social stability; later the promotion of materialistic values would be added to the list. Children learned to read aloud and to spell. They learned what was correct and what was incorrect. In language instruction they learned the arbitrary injunctions of the grammar books, what things they should say and write, and what they should avoid, and they did this within a rigid, moral climate in which the Bible eventually gave some ground to secular morality. Authority was all around them, from Noah Webster's blue-backed spellers to the moral conclusions that they were required to draw from every writer they were allowed to read. Literacy became a "social good" and illiteracy became tied to poverty, idleness, crime, and drunkenness.

Literacy continued to spread but, even when literacy is defined quite minimally by the ability to sign a marriage register, it was not universal in England until the beginning of the twentieth century. One can argue that mass literacy has never been an easily attainable goal. Literacy must bring benefits to those who want to become literate. The benefits of literacy in the nineteenth century would not have been obvious to many who went to school. What they learned may also not have left a very deep impression.

Such observations remain true in the twentieth century. The middle classes see education as bringing salvation to those below them. However, these would-be beneficiaries may have a different view. Paul Roberts, writing in *The Classic Slum*, an account of life in Salford in the first quarter of the twentieth century, says of the working-class experience of schooling of that time: "With a deep consciousness of global possession, a grasp of the decalogue and a modicum of knowledge we left in droves at the very first hour the law would allow." He adds: "Most men struggling for a living knew well enough that for them literacy bought no bread," and that although there might be a few books in many houses, particularly books like *Uncle Tom's Cabin*, *The Old Curiosity Shop*, and *Black Beauty*, acquired through attendance at Sunday scools, "many of our sub-literates treasured these books, but, I discovered, seldom read them. They stood on the chiffonier as ornaments and were not looked upon as objects to be handled. Children were even forbidden to touch them."

In Richard Hoggart's *The Uses of Literacy*, we see a similar less-than-optimistic account of the consequences of education and literacy. In his description of popular working-class culture in England in the first half of the twentieth century, Hoggart points out the various paradoxes and confusions that surround literacy: the pull between the oral and the literate traditions, the mixture of old ways and new, the places of skepticism and belief, the roles of private and public pleasures, and the tension that existed between "us" and "them." Such people as those that Hoggart writes about may not necessarily be pulled inevitably toward "higher things." They may resent being viewed as objects to be controlled and manipulated. They have certainly proved resistant to some of the moral injunctions that they have been subjected to for generations, but then they have never been accustomed to seeing these same injunctions observed by those who preached them. So that is an entirely sensible reaction!

There is a paradox in the whole effort to elevate the masses through education. Improving the masses might tend to decrease social distance. Undoubtedly there has been some decrease in such distance over the last century or two. However, smaller differences then become very important. In a society in which there are vast differences and everyone knows everyone's place you can still, like Harold Macmillan, British Prime Minister from 1957 to 1963, use *it don't*, but in one in which there is less distance and a greater possibility of movement small differences become extremely important. For those who profess to care about such matters, education, particularly language education, has now become obsessed with trivia in a way that it has never been: we are constantly informed that the graduates of our schools cannot spell, cannot write, speak badly, and do not know their "grammar." But how many such claims can actually be substantiated and how important are the various matters in which the young are said to be deficient? We need to give serious thought to questions such as these.

5 The Perseverance of Oral Culture

We must not ignore our rich oral culture if we want to understand how language functions in our lives. Oral culture predated written culture, a rather late-comer on the human stage. In the western world oral culture and the oral tradition associated with it no longer have the prestige of matters that have been committed to writing but in many other societies they are still the major sources of "truth." A tradition associated with an oral culture has virtues as well as drawbacks. We tend to see only the latter. An oral tradition is infinitely malleable in that each generation can mold it to meet its needs. A written tradition lacks that flexibility; writing lends an authority that is not easily challenged or changed. An oral tradition is an immediate public one: it belongs to everyone and is "alive." On the other hand, a written tradition is private and "fixed," and it tends to encourage disputes over "ownership," even ownership of the very means of transmission itself, i.e., language.

Initially, the invention of printing and the acquisition of literacy by a few had little impact on most people's lives. The acquisition of literacy does not silence oral culture; it can provide people with something quite fresh to talk about. There is still a need to learn how to do things by doing them; learning from books does not suddenly replace that kind of learning. Literacy can give people new insights in learning how to cope with the world and enlarge older understandings and beliefs. The skills of literacy tended to supplement "oral literacy" rather than replace it. Here, for example, is a selection of some of the titles hawked by pedlars in England in 1566 among a whole selection of fables, romances, recipes, histories, almanacs, religious tracts, herbals, ballads, sermons, and lives, particularly lives of saints: *News out of India, A Powder to kill worms, A Water to make the Skin fair, A Preservative against the Plague, Merry Tales,* and *Songs and Ballets.* Other broadsheets of the period included *The true description of two monstrous children born at Herne in Kent* of 1565, *The description of a rare or rather monstrous fish taken on the east coast of Holland* of 1566, and *A notable and prodigious history of a maiden (C. Cooper) who for sundry years neither eats, drinks nor sleeps* of 1589.

Popular culture has long been one in which organized religion, formal education, the fine arts, and belles lettres have had no place. Instead, it is a culture of folk songs and folk tales, of wakes, festivals, carnivals, and fairs, of itinerant players, teachers, and healers, of magic and witchcraft, of icons, images, and shrines, of mystery plays, farces, jugglers, minstrels, and acrobats, of bear-baiting, cock-fighting, card-playing and wagering, and of almanacs, pamphlets, cheap newspapers, broadsides and chapbooks. It is both a peasant culture and a town culture, with its meeting places public rather than private: the market place, the tavern, and the guild, union, or association. It is a culture of periodic licensed disorder and one of occasional riot and rebellion. Within it there is a strong anti-authoritarian streak which shows up in the mockery of authority and the glorification of folk heroes such as Robin Hood, Dick Turpin, and Captain Kidd. Authorities have always found much in all of the above to disapprove of, even ban if they could. They opposed these un-Christian, pagan, heretical, riotous, ribald, and immoral activities and believed that education and religion would save people from them.

Developments in the nineteenth century may have broadened the gap between popular culture and high culture. Certainly by the end of the century it was much easier to distinguish those who used standard English from those who did not, those who knew some Latin from those who did not, those who pursued high culture in its various forms in education, science, the arts, and literature from those who did not. In England at least there were "two nations" so distinguished.

The nineteenth century was a time in which some people read Darwin's *Voyage of The Beagle* and the works of Dickens as they were published, classics such as *Pilgrim's Progress, Gulliver's Travels, Journal of the Plague Year, The Mill on the Floss,* and *The Vicar of Wakefield,* and the poetry of Wordsworth and later of Tennyson. However, it was also the era of the gutter press and of an *Account of a Dreadful and Horrible Murder committed by Mary Bell Upon the Body of Her Mother, an arsenic killing,* of *Evelina, the Pauper's Child; or, Poverty, Crime, and Sorrow, A Romance of Deep Pathos,* a "gothic" with a happy ending, and of various best sellers about assorted thieves, murderers, and seducers, including among these the notorious Sweeney Todd, the demon barber of Fleet Street.

Our rich, oral tradition continues and popular culture prospers. Formal education tends to ignore them just as they ignore formal education. The mass media and the ready availabilty of print and the spoken word on radio and television serve as much to rein-force the old ways as to undermine them. What we are witness-ing today is a reshaping of old ways not a sea change.

A century or more of mass education leaves much unchanged in our lives. Superstition and even witchcraft in one form or an-other abound. Millions today do not know the difference between astrology and astronomy, much preferring the claims of the former to the findings of the latter. There are new cults and gurus every-where. People believe in UFOs, psychic powers, angels, Satan, ghosts, charms, spells, the magical powers of crystals and pyra-mids, miracles, lucky and unlucky numbers, exorcism, and so on, and such beliefs sometimes find "official" acceptance. Scientific findings, on the other hand, are likely to get short shrift. People often do not understand elementary facts about how their bodies work or the nature of disease, and dangerous beliefs about how to prevent or cure this or that illness are much in evidence. There are also the self-appointed advisors, those who tell you about what the stars have in store for you, or how to change your lifestyle, or win the lottery, or dip into your previous lives, or make a for-tune. And people riot and destroy things periodically, and not just after sporting events.

Education and literacy allow people to read but they do not necessarily read a great deal. When they do read, they also read material that is different from what they read in school. The masses read the tabloids, posters, drug-store books, and popular maga-zines. They read articles in the sensational press with titles like *Your co-worker may be a space alien, Princess Grace alive!, Mermaid eaten by hungry fisherman, Our toilet is haunted by a plumber's ghost,* and *Bigfoot is the father of my child.* We must compare the current popularity of the tabloids, Harlequin Romances, and authors such as Michael Crichton, Barbara Cartland, John Grisham, Danielle Steel, and Jeffrey Archer with that of the quality newspapers and the literary classics. Who reads Proust and Joyce? How many read-ers finished Stephen Hawking's *A Brief History of Time*? Does it matter if the answer is few? Would the world be a better place if we read Proust as eagerly as we read Stephen King?

Literacy may have fragmented modern life, pitting those who prize it against those who do not. It may have set home against school, the practical against the theoretical, "low" culture against "high" culture, the oral against the written, and the popular against the literary. This great cultural divide helps to explain why the language goes its own merry way in the mouths of the masses; the concerns that a few have about it are unlikely to change what utters forth from those mouths.

6 The Legacy of Literacy

Literacy is an important issue in the modern world. Governments almost everywhere try to raise the level of literacy in their peoples. Some observers have gone so far as to claim that the introduction of writing has transformed that world indelibly. In this view writing made modern types of civilization possible. This is another chicken-and-egg argument. One cannot exist without the other, or, in I. J. Gelb's heavily emphasized words in *A Study of Writing*, *"Writing exists only in a civilization and a civilization cannot exist without writing."*

Some writers maintain that the key invention that transformed the human race was not so much writing as either the development of the alphabet or the technological innovation of printing. Jack Goody, the anthropologist, says as much in *Literacy in Traditional Societies*. Others are Marshall McLuhan, the media guru, in *The Gutenberg Galaxy*, Eric Havelock, the classicist, in *The Literate Revolution in Greece and its Cultural Consequences*, and Robert Logan, a physicist and disciple of McLuhan, in *The Alphabet Effect*. Havelock, for example, described the Greek alphabet as "a piece of explosive technology, revolutionary in its effects on human culture, in a way not precisely shared by any other invention" and added that it "furnished a necessary conceptual foundation on which to build the structures of the modern sciences and philosophies." The alphabet allowed people to study language itself. Logan maintains that alphabets promote the use of abstract, logical, and theoretical thought whereas writing systems like those used by the Chinese encourage the concrete and the practical. In such a view, the alphabet gave the West a vital edge in the world, one responsible for the development of science and logic and even of the concepts of "individuality," "codified law," and "monotheism." While such claims are challenging, they are unscientific because there is no possible way of disproving them. They are articles of faith not scientific propositions. That literate people are somehow more "logical" than non-literate people is particularly hard to accept.

A contrasting view is one that Robert Pattison expresses in *On Literacy:* "Writing did not make the Greek mind skeptical, logical, historical, or democratic. Instead it furnished an opportunity for these predispositions to flourish." Pattison denies that print "created a mass audience that was disciplined, studious, and vigorous in the championship of humane ideals" or that Europeans adopted "a scientific and realistic attitude toward life, learned self-reliance, and gained perspective, all from the suddenly acquired habit of looking at neatly justified pages of print." He adds: "Nothing of the sort happened." The introduction of printing coincided with a transformation of the world into which it was introduced. That world changed from "medieval" to "modern," from largely oral to heavily literary in tradition, from the freedom of individual writing to the uniform demands of the printed page, from the pre-scientific to the scientific, and from pre-capitalistic organization to a system that required the accumulation of capital. However, it may not have been the cause of any one of these so much as just another change typical of the whole process of change that was occurring at the time.

Writing acts as a conservative force in society. Writing has an air of authority about it; literate cultures exalt the written word: "Put that in writing", "What does the dictionary say?", "How does the law read?" The written word also becomes very difficut to change. Religious texts, laws, books, and records become permanent, authoritative sources. So much is written these days, and written matter quickly becomes something in its own right, spinning off whole new worlds of possibility for comparison, exegesis, and dispute. Non-literate cultures are not so fixated.

States and other authorities have always sought some measure of control over print, trying to regulate this, promote that, or prohibit the other. The latest such issue is the amount of control, if any, that should be exercised over the internet. It is much more difficult to behave like this with the spoken word. Authorities try to control print because people put a great deal of trust in those things that do get into print, partly as a result of how they acquire literacy. *I saw it in the paper today* or *But the dictionary says so!* are just two of the kinds of statements we hear.

Writing has the psychological effect of suggesting standards, permanence, and authority in a way that speech does not. Speech is transient, changing, democratic, and "vulgar" in the original sense of that word. As the authority of the spoken language has given way before the authority of the written language now it is the spoken language that is little valued. No more do we have great orators and epic poets. Now we have the prepared statement, the diplomatic note, the written brief, and the final report.

The residues of the older way are few but we see them on occasion. Laws are proclaimed. A change of monarch in the United Kingdom has its spoken formula: *The king/queen is dead; long live the king/queen!*. The Riot Act is read or crowds are threatened by being told that it will be read. The United States Congress has much material "read into its record."

In these last examples we also see how the spoken language and reading are commingled. Reading was once oral performance. Everyone read aloud and silent reading is a late-comer on the scene. If reading aloud is in one way a continuation of the old oral tradition, it also changes that tradition because it introduces the notion of "correct reading" and, in doing so, elevates the written language over the spoken language as a source of authority .

Writing undoubtedly brings about the accumulation of knowledge, the development of literary traditions, and the study of language itself. It vastly increases the possible uses of language. There can be no equivalent in the spoken language for encyclopedias, dictionaries, grammars, bills of lading, complex scientific formulas, sophisticated graphics, and the vast array of signs and notices we encounter these days. All of these are important in modern society. In this respect at least the written and the spoken language differ dramatically and the written language is far from being merely a representation of the spoken language.

The permanence of such artefacts is also important. They require standards in their execution and impose uniformity. There are right ways and wrong ways of doing things. Once we develop such an attitude it may become difficult for us to accept any changes that are occurring. Change appears to undermine the standards we have achieved sometimes at great cost.

Education into literacy becomes education into certain practices and standards. For some this is a very liberating experience; I can speak to that from personal knowledge. However, I also know that it may be difficult, if not impossible, for many. As Stephen Pinker says in *The Language Instinct*, "Expository writing requires language to express more complex trains of thought than it was biologically designed to do." There is something unnatural about the process. Acquiring standard English and the "right" accent to go with it may be just as daunting. Education that has such goals is by no means "neutral." It is also an education into a common morality and one that requires us to show respect for particular types of authority. If we seek to play this game, we must learn its rules and to obey these. It is a game that serves the ends of powerful interest groups and of the state. Not all seek to play.

We are told that today there is a decline in literacy in many western countries. That may or may not be the case. What we may actually be seeing is the failure of the above program. Literacy is not easy to advance or even maintain if there is little worthwhile to read or if what is available to read is largely irrelevant to potential readers. Teaching people to read does not necessarily make them avid readers and encourage an appetite for learning. Literacy may lead some to reject the idea of learning altogether. Or it may open up other ways of pursuing the so-called "disreputable pleasures," which, after all, have always been with us.

Does literacy inevitably open up new worlds to all those who acquire an ability to decipher written texts? It is hard to prove that it does, and it probably cannot if those new worlds are of little interest or cannot be entered. The way literacy is taught too, particularly the way in which language is used in that teaching, does not liberate. Favoring myths about language rather than facts and authority rather than reason, it must accept some of the responsibility for the failures we perceive. How we "learn" people their language explains much about the attitudes they have toward it.

CHAPTER SEVEN

Learning
about **English**

The beginings of our western tradition of scientific inquiry are found in ancient Greece. As Leonard Bloomfield wrote in *Language*, "The ancient Greeks had the gift of wondering at things that other people take for granted." They were interested in the world around them and in natural phenomena. They asked questions and sought answers, and they gave some of this attention to language. However, the tradition of language study they began has had many stops and starts. The Greeks gave it a strong initial impetus, but then it languished for two millennia until once again coming to life in the nineteenth century. As Holger Pedersen said in the first sentence of *The Discovery of Language*, "Until the close of the eighteenth century, European linguistic science had advanced but little beyond the knowledge of linguistics achieved by the Greeks and Romans." There is a more recent view expressed by Derek Bickerton in *Language and Species*: "Most of what we know about language has been learned in the last three decades." How much do we know about language, and why is the general public so badly informed about language matters?

1 Language Study and Linguistics

There are various histories of the development of linguistics, but a caveat is in order. Historical works are always informed by ideologies. We write history anew each generation from the perspective of our current interests and concerns. We do the same for the history of laguage study. For example, we see the development of literacy from the concerns of our own day. All histories are selective and we can see this principle at work in overviews of language study as dissimilar as the first chapter of Bloomfield's *Language*, Frederick Newmayer's *Linguistic Theory in America*, and Noam Chomsky's *Cartesian Linguistics*.

Bickerton can say what he says because the topics that interest him in the study of language have seemed approachable only in the last three decades or so. Earlier, a few people were interested in the same topics but lacked some of the means we have for dealing with them. To Bickerton it is apparent that every significant advance has been a recent development. By adopting this attitude, he dismisses the work of generations of language scholars, work that would have made an enormous difference if it had been able to effect meaningful changes in the long tradition of language study within which so many of us have been educated.

One general statement we can make about the study of language matters is that it swings between periods of close observation of phenomena and others in which the quest for universal truth is more noticeable. For example, during the 1960s American linguistics swung from interests of the first kind to those of the second. Observation and speculation have always been countervailing forces in the study of language. Unfortunately, for the longest time people did not know what to make of their observations and saw only disorder. Their reliance on Latin severely limited the possibilities they could consider and its importance so dominated their thinking that they were unable to treat languages such as English in an insightful manner.

We know that there was a wide range of interest in the English language in the seventeenth and eighteenth centuries. In the seventeenth century there was a strong interest in the nature of language, the possibility of improving languages, and the various uses of language. In the eighteenth century the concern turned mainly to "fixing" language. This concern with achieving certainty was so important that it met with some success: a single variety of English was given approval in a specific, written form. From that time on, the study of English could not ignore that single, approved variety, *because that was what English was*. Frozen with it were attitudes about the nature of language and how we should talk about language.

One serious consequence that lasts to this day and affects current linguistic study is the focus placed on this standard, written variety and how it is pronounced. Although there are studies of different dialects and of nonstandard speech and writing, most linguistic scholarship on English is concerned with standard English. But should this fact be so surprising? Professional linguists themselves are usually educated, literate people. They feel most comfortable discussing the variety of English they know best while giving a nod occasionally to other varieties. In doing so, they also do not upset others. Far better to work with edited prose, with the niceties of formal speech, and with the notion of "language competence" than with the superficial disorder of conversation, dialect variation, and all the complexities and messiness of actual "language performance."

Modern linguistics grew out of the study of philology that followed the important discovery of the relationship of Sanskrit to languages such as Greek and Latin. The main locus of linguistics in the nineteenth century was in Germany and this linguistics was almost entirely historical and comparative in nature. One outgrowth was a new account of the histories of various words and sounds as linguists gained a better understanding of the historical development of languages and of the relationships among languages. However, this knowledge was not welcome everywhere; Noah Webster, for example, resisted until the very last revising any of his etymologies to conform to the new discoveries because he distrusted this new German science.

In 1786 Sir William Jones, a British judge schooled in Greek and Latin and interested in the languages of India where he served the crown, announced to the Royal Asiatic Society in Calcutta that there was such an "affinity" among Greek, Latin, and Sanskrit that they must all have "sprung from some common source, which, perhaps, no longer exists." This discovery of the importance of Sanskrit led to the discovery of the linguistic work of Panini and other linguists of ancient India. However, it was their work on Sanskrit phonetics rather than on Sanskrit grammar that most interested linguists. The Sanskrit linguists had been concerned with maintaining the accuracy of the pronunciation and understanding of the Vedic hymns and prayers, the sacred texts of their culture, which were an essential part of Brahman rituals. Modern linguists found their phonetic observations invaluable in coming to a better understanding of the properties of spoken languages. This understanding was necessary in order to achieve a further understanding of the relationship of speech and writing and to challenge the widely-held belief that writing acted as a guide to speaking.

Aa it is practiced at the end of the twentieth century, linguistics owes much to three different component strands. The first is the historical work of the nineteenth and early twentieth century. The second is the descriptive work of the mid-twentieth century. The third, developed in the later part of the twentieth century, is a focus on more abstract, universal issues.

The historical work revealed the major relationships among languages in the world. In doing so, it established families of languages and provided a systematic account of how languages change and differentiate over time and space. It also helped to shed light on the concepts of "language" and "dialect." Tremendous strides were made in such historical work in collecting and organizing data, particularly historical data. Out of it came dictionaries such as the *OED*, historical grammars, and histories of particular language families and of individual languages. Greek and Latin were "put in their place" in this work: they were just languages like all others. However, these languages did not lose their hold on the western imagination. They did not because their hold was a wider, cultural one not a linguistic one alone.

In the descriptive phase, largely prompted by the theorizings of Ferdinand de Saussure, Edward Sapir, and Leonard Bloomfield, linguists turned their attention to describing many of the languages of the world using a set of basic linguistic concepts such as the "phoneme," the "morpheme," and "constituency." Languages were described on their own terms, i.e., without recourse to a Latinate model. Moreover, considerable emphasis was placed on describing previously unwritten languages and on the spoken varieties of written languages. The result was a set of completely new accounts of languages, particularly accounts of various aspects of English, which often differed dramatically from existing Latinate accounts, used different terminology, were concerned with different phenomena from traditional accounts, e.g., the spoken language, and refused to acknowledge that native speakers of a language could be ungrammatical. This work was widely asssailed outside linguistics because it seemed to ignore traditional "standards" and be anarchic in intent. Some critics went so far as to declare that it was deliberately directed toward ruining the language. For example, Robert Hall's book *Leave Your Language Alone!*, later in 1960 more wisely retitled *Linguistics and Your Language*, provoked strong negative criticism when it first appeared in 1950. The same critics also regarded *Webster's Third* as a prototypical product of this approach to language.

In the late twentieth century Noam Chomsky's theoretical work shifted the emphasis of much linguistic inquiry toward fundamental issues concerning the nature of language and what the structure of language can tell us about the human mind. It redirected attention toward properties that all languages share and the issue of how language might have arisen in the human species and even when it might have arisen. All languages appear to be fundamentally alike just as are all minds. There are local variations that we must explain but general processes of language acquisition and language change can account for these.

In this view differences among languages are largely superficial and differences among individual users of a specific language are trivial. Of course, that is not the popular view because we have been brought up to believe that such differences are important. If, as a consequence of our acculturation, we believe that Latin is better than English or the language of the Queen of England is better than our own, that tells something about the way we have been brought up and nothing very interesting about language itself.

Linguistics today is not an entirely uniform discipline, one in which the practitioners speak with a single voice. To some outsiders it seems to be rent right down the middle according to whether individual linguists do or do not subscribe to Chomsky's views and then into further sub-groupings. Such differences have led some observers to conclude that linguistics is so seriously flawed that it may safely be ignored. That is entirely the wrong conclusion to draw, for behind the differences there is a remarkable uniformity of views that we cannot ignore.

Linguists agree that all languages have grammars that are extraordinarily complex. Moreover, we do not have anywhere a complete grammar of a single language, that is a grammar that tells us unequivocally how native speakers of that language construct sentences and tells us infallibly why a particular sentence in that language is grammatical and some other possibility – theoretical possibility at least – is ungrammatical. Speakers of the language have that ability and any grammar we construct for a language should account for it in an interesting way.

Linguists believe that speakers of any language use a set of rules and principles to create sentences in that language and that the set of sentences such rules and principles allow is infinite. A grammar of a language must account for this ability that speakers have. The grammar cannot be no more than a simple listing of word classes and constructions because it must also tell us how these word classes relate to one another and what exactly are constructions in the language. Moreover, it should do this within a framework which at the same time allows us to understand how a pre-literate three-year-old is able to demonstrate this very same ability.

What we are concerned with is an abstract knowledge that allows the speaker of a language to create and understand new sentences in that language. The knowledge is knowledge of rules and principles of some kind, but what are these? Furthermore, it is knowledge that all speakers of the language share. That is what it means to "know" the grammar of a language. This knowledge is not something we find written in the grammars to which we have been accustomed. Three-year-olds possess it to a remarkable degree and almost all three-year-olds are illiterate. Everyone who speaks a language "knows" the rules and principles of that language. The linguist's task is to try to find what these are and perhaps describe them in a "grammar." While such a grammar might have some value in *teaching about* the language, it is doubtful that it will have any value in *teaching* the language. It is also true that the traditional accounts we have of English meet neither such requirement.

Whatever a grammar of a language is, it is largely impervious to human intervention. That is, the really interesting rules and principles are so basic that we cannot do anything at all about them. What we can do is try to influence some of the minor outcomes, for example, try to insist that people say *I drank* instead of *I drunk* or *It's I* instead of *It's me*. Essentially that is tinkering with matters of no linguistic consequence. To elevate the study of grammar to the task of trying to bring about "correction" in such matters is to trivialize that study. These matters may be of social consequence and often are, but that is a social observation not a linguistic one, because *I drunk* and *It's me* are linguistically on a par with *I drank* and *It's I*. Furthermore, it is an observation that tells us much about social organization and the function of trivia in such organization and nothing about the structure of language.

Whereas everyone who speaks a language draws on a grammar of that language, there are often local variations in some of its details. Many such differences are related to regional and social groupings of speakers of the language, giving us regional and social dialects. Linguistically, these differences are interesting because they enable us to see how different groups handle certain details of the grammar. No group can be said to handle such details "better" or "worse" than any other group. What we do observe, however, is that the solutions of one group may be more highly valued than those of other groups and deemed superior. Once again this is a social judgment not a linguistic one. In English the double-negative solution to the problem of negation is just as "good" or "bad" as the single-negative solution – the French might even say it is "better," possibly even "more logical," because standard French requires both *ne* and *pas* – but it is the single-negative solution that wins the cultured vote in English.

Languages change constantly. Although change is inevitable, its course in a particular language is largely unpredictable. Languages seem to live lives of their own that are independent of those who speak them. We know from historical changes that have occurred in languages we have studied that some changes take centuries to work through. Individual speakers get caught up in changes they are not aware of. They are not conscious of change nor can they be sure that they are in a period of slow or

the time of Virgil and Cicero. Their languages are just as "old" as Latin, which anyway is now French, Spanish, Italian, etc.

Linguists now have a good idea of the relationship of speaking and writing. Languages are basically spoken phenomena. Writing evolved as a way of giving some kind of permanence to speech. There are different writing systems and these are of three kinds: logographic, representing something we might call whole words; syllabic, representing syllables; and alphabetic, representing individual sounds. (We might add that "word," "syllable," and "sound" themselves are very puzzling linguistic concepts.)

Writing is a relatively recent invention but one that has taken a strong hold on the human imagination, so strong in fact that it has distorted our view of the very nature of language. When linguists assign a primacy to the study of speech, they are reminding us of a basic fact about language. They are not saying that writing is unimportant. Writing is very important but it is not the whole of language: it is a part and a derivative part at that.

Linguists find that all languages and all varieties of a language are equally interesting to study. All languages and varieties are equal in their eyes. They are equal as objects of scientific study; we can learn as much about the nature of language from one as from another. The statement does not mean that all languages are equal in the uses that people have made of them. Some have writing systems; others do not. Some are standardized; others are not. Some are associated with complex modern cultures; others are not. Some have long attested histories; others do not. Some are used by many millions of people; others are used by only a handful. Languages are unequal in these respects. However, no language or variety of a language is inherently incapable of rising to the full range of possibilities and uses of an "advantaged" language in the world, e.g., of a language like English, French, or Japanese. Moreover, even a thoroughly "disadvantaged" language is too complex for the most sophisticated linguists today to understand in its entirety. There are no such things as "primitive" languages.

Languages tend to reflect the uses their speakers find for them in the societies that use them. They develop vocabulary to reflect the concerns of these societies. Some would go further to say that

165

each language imposes on its speakers a particular "world view," but it is much more likely that people use the language they have to demonstrate a particular world view. A language is not inherently sexist; rather those that use it have "sexist" attitudes and use language to support them.

Finally, attitudes and beliefs, whether sexist or linguistic, are learned during the process of acculturation. Language is learned – or rather acquired – in an entirely different way. A first language is learned just as walking is learned: in normal circumstances we cannot really avoid learning a language, it takes little or no conscious effort, and direct teaching is almost completely irrelevant. However, attitudes toward, and beliefs about, language are learned. Along with acquiring language goes a whole lot of instruction about language, instruction that inevitably leads us to believe this or that and develop attitudes toward our language and the languages of others. Part of our knowledge of language is knowledge of what we have been told about that language, right or wrong.

Much of the instruction about language that we experience is false or misleading in its content. Many of the beliefs we acquire about language cannot be supported by facts. Much that we have come to believe to be true about language is false. Linguists know that this is so. They know that this is also a fact about language but a fact of a different order from those they are concerned with. Their usual response is to point out how misinformed most people are on linguistic matters. Most tend to try to avoid any further discussion, having learned still another fact: false beliefs are so deeply ingrained that they are almost unchangeable.

One consequence is that linguists usually talk almost exclusively to other linguists about what they know. The academic discipline has its own interests, structure, jargon, and independence. Most linguists now feel quite comfortable working almost exclusively within a narrow, academic discipline but one that has grown rapidly in the twentieth century. Not a few linguists remember how those who have tried to popularize linguistic ideas have been treated not only by people outside the discipline but also on occasion by some within. It is dangerous to try to debunk erroneous ideas outside the discipline because those who have such ideas often hold powerful positions in the media, and the "popularizers" of almost any discipline are often not highly regarded, even by those whose work they try to make accessible to the general public. In such circumstances we must count ourselves fortunate to have such books as Dwight Bolinger's *Language the Loaded Weapon*, David Crystal's *Who Cares about English Usage?*, and Randolph Quirk's *The Use of English*.

The jargon of modern linguistics has not helped the cause either. Some jargon is necessary because jargon is, in at least one of its meanings, the technical language of a particular calling. However, some linguists do seem to have created new linguistic terms almost for the sake of creating terms, and there has been on occasion some poor writing. Linguists are certainly not alone when it comes to such matters; much scholarly writing seems almost by definition to have to be dull and dreary.

The establishment of linguistics as a separate discipline has, paradoxically, once again left the field of language commentary wide open to anyone who wants to enter, most linguists having withdrawn to their own separate pasture, realizing after the debacle following the publication of *Webster's Third* that, in the words of a 1964 report to a National Commission on the Humanities by the American Council of Learned Societies, "the impact which the recent advances in linguistics have had upon the the general public [is] essentially zero." This situation is largely unchanged today in North America, so anyone can now comment on language matters and be fairly confident of being left alone by linguists. Many such commentators take a certain pride in deliberately ignoring the findings of linguistics. When we hear and read popular accounts of language matters, we could well believe that nobody has given a serious thought to language matters for generations. Self-proclaimed experts are everywhere but most of that expertise is just a rehash of the old mumbo-jumbo. Linguistic scholarship is ignored.

2 The Failure of Language Teaching

There can hardly be another subject in the school curriculum in North America on which so many hours have been spent with such poor results as teaching about the English language. In reading instruction, grammatical study, or composition, this teaching has been so filled with error and misunderstanding that, as often as not, it has harmed rather than helped learners. Teaching about language is undoubtedly one of the leading causes of people not being interested in language.

Much of the language teaching we have experienced has bred nothing but uncertainty and doubt about language. We are more likely to have acquired ideas language that are false than any that might contain a germ of truth. We will almost certainly have gained no understanding of what language is, of what grammars and rules are, about how languages vary and change, about the relationship of speech to writing, and about the origins and nature of reference books on language. Instead, we will have been indoctrinated into a set of beliefs about much of the above, beliefs that breed insecurity in our use of language.

Many teachers have come to suspect that this kind of traditional language study has been inadequate without necessarily understanding why it is so. Consequently, they have simply eliminated any systematic study of language from what they do in classrooms. This has been the principal reason behind removing the study of grammar from so many schools. Once Latin was dropped as a subject, the teaching of traditional grammar became a complete waste of time. The grammar of English could have become a subject of inquiry in schools but linguistically-oriented approaches were never adopted. Latin and Latinate grammars of English went out and nothing replaced them.

Linguists have sometimes been blamed for this decline in the teaching of grammar and for a perceived accompanying decline in "standards." The truth is that most schools have almost completely ignored linguistic findings. They threw out the old grammar and involved themselves with social and cultural issues, it being much easier to try to foster "creativitity" and "self-expression," whatever these are, than to insist on a rigorous study of language – or, in some cases, a rigorous study of anything at all. Schools reflect society; they do not mold it.

What we are left with then is a vacuum. There is little serious study of language in the schools. Latinate grammars should have no place because we do not teach Latin any more. However, we still use the terminology from those grammars when we talk about language. Many of the beliefs we have about language are those of earlier times. Teachers hold these beliefs just as members of the wider public do, and we continue to hand them down from generation to generation.

The situation seems to be less bleak in the United Kingdom. One of the great controversies in education in England and Wales in the 1980s and early 1990s was over language teaching in the schools – or a perceived lack of it. Margaret Thatcher, the Prince of Wales, and Jeffrey Archer were just three representative critics among many who deplored how the English language was either taught or ignored. The critics wanted more teaching of grammar. Even though the Bullock Report of 1975, the Kingman Report of 1988, and the Cox Report of 1989 had each in its way found little merit in these critics' arguments, conservative forces rallied round the idea that more teaching of grammar was necessary to ensure not just a better educated populace but a more disciplined one with more "character" and less "sloppiness." In order to make such a program work, the new National Curriculum, John Marenbon, an influential conservative thinker, declared that teachers needed to know "traditional grammar," which they would teach to children in their charge. That apparently was to be the key to solving both language and social problems.

The critics did not get their way. Linguists were able to influence the choices that were made and as a consequence have been more influential with school authorities in the United Kingdom than they have been in North America. There is an English language syllabus which shows the influence of modern ideas about language, there are books and materials available for school use, and there are linguists who are willing to spend time with teachers and students. As we have seen, attitudes toward language in the United Kingdom have never been as inflexible as those in North America so it is not surprising to see these signs of progress.

The key to changing what happens in schools is the training of those who teach in them. We might expect that good training in matters to do with language would help teachers do a better job everywhere. However, a training only in traditional grammar might be counter-productive because of its irrelevance. What are the chances of any teacher getting a good training in language? In 1925 Leonard Bloomfield, in a paper that tried to answer the question "Why a Linguistic Society?," declared that: "Our schools are conducted by persons who, from professors of education down to teachers in the classroom, know nothing of the results of linguistic science, not even the relation of writing to speech or of standard language to dialect. In short, they do not know what language is, and yet they must teach it . . . ." Three-quarters of a century have passed since Bloomfield wrote those words but the situation he refers to remains unchanged in many parts of the English-speaking world.

Teachers of beginning reading, even those trained in phonics, too often have no clear idea about the relationship of the spoken to the written language, do not understand the sound system of English, misunderstand what children "know" about their language, have no concept of dialect variation, and fail to see the vicious circularity in much of what they try to teach. We should not be surprised that there is such a controversy between the "phonics" and "look-and-say" approaches to beginning reading when both kinds of instruction are so filled with misunderstandings. Yet that need not be so.

We might expect teachers of English at the secondary level to be better informed and professors of English to know something about what they profess, the English language. They are usually the products of our college and university departments of English and should be well informed on language matters. However, that is also often not the case. The one subject we can be almost sure that is not studied in depth in many such departments is the English language; it actually gets short shrift in many such places. There may be some study of Old English and Middle English so that a favored few can read *Beowulf* and Chaucer. There may be a course on the history of the English language but it is likely to concentrate on superficial matters. However, courses requiring students of English to take a serious look at how the English language works or at matters of usage – as opposed to style – will almost certainly be conspicuously absent from departmental offerings.

The Department of English of the University of Toronto, Canada's largest university, is a good exemplar of this disreregrd of the language. With about a hundred active professorial appointees, it offers a like number of undergraduate and graduate courses with perhaps half a dozen of these having anything directly to do with language. In the university the single course on the structure of the English language is offered in another department entirely and only rarely does a student from the English department take it. This is not surprising. Did not the English department's best-known professor, the literary critic Northrop Frye, write as follows in a foreword to a history of his department: "The enrooting of English study in Latin still went on in my time, and some of its benefits were very considerable. My own elementary school (New Brunswick in the early twenties) afforded only a few paradigms of Latin and some moralizing junk that passed for literature, but it also had Latinate English grammar, with the categories and organizing conceptions of English derived from Latin. How I could ever have got anywhere as a writer without that training I don't know. The linguists say that this kind of grammar is all wrong, but I was lucky enough to live before the linguists"?

There is a reason for such neglect. English departments in colleges and universities, like all other departments there that carry language names, are departments devoted almost entirely to the study of literature rather than language. Today, you gain more academic mileage in an English department by studying some esoteric theory of criticism or some obscure, medieval poet than by trying to wrestle with the complexities of how you and your students are using the language to communicate. As Mark Turner says in *Reading Minds*, "University researchers and scholars have become sophisticated in every fashionable new field in our profession as currently constituted, but a harsh critic might say that we have regressed in our knowledge of what will always be the logical core of this profession: the elementary arts of language." Surprisingly, but then perhaps not so if we really think about it, the exceptions are found in English departments in the non-English speaking world. Some of most informed discussion of the English language has come out of countries such as the Netherlands, Denmark, Germany, and Poland.

Our English departments produce our researchers in English and our teachers of English, and many of our writers have graduated from them too. One consequence is that they graduate profoundly ignorant in language matters. Steeped in one or other aspect of English literature, they have absorbed the prejudices of the past about language in general and the English language in particular. These are not prejudices to them; they are truths they are quite prepared to hand on to others. Consequently, almost nothing changes in English departments, in our schools, and in the comments of those who find themselves in a position to influence others about language matters. There is hardly any other area in life in which people so badly informed can actually be proud of their ignorance while still proclaiming themselves to be guardians of truth and saviors of others from error.

In the United States an important body of English teachers tried for years to change the way that language was viewed in classrooms. The National Council of Teachers of English (NCTE) was founded in 1911 and from the beginning a number of professors trained in linguistics were influential in its activities. The NCTE went so far as to sponsor a series of studies of the language and publish their results in the hope that certain practices deemed harmful to students would be changed.

The first such study was Sterling Leonard's *Current English Usage* of 1932. He had previously published *The Doctrine of Correctness in English Usage 1700–1800* in 1929. In that work, commenting on expressions such as *ain't* and *you was*, which he acknowledged to be of long standing in the language, Leonard said that "so long as feeling against a usage in fact exists, young people need to know this as a protection against the prejudices which its use may arouse against them." In *Current English Usage* Leonard examined the linguistic usage of different groups of people, e.g., linguists, authors, businessmen, editors, and teachers, and asked them to report on whether or not they used certain expressions. He then classified these expressions, 230 altogether, as "established," "disputable," or "illiterate." In the first category he placed such usages as *None of them are here*, *It is me*, and *Who are you looking for?* In the second category we find *Everybody bought their own ticket* and *He dove off the pier*, and in the third *The data is often inaccurate*. Leonard recommended that teachers accept the usages he had labeled "established" and recognize the currency of those labeled "disputable," declaring that dogmatism about these is unjustified. Teachers should continue to reject those usages he had labeled as "illiterate." Leonard wanted teachers to try to encourage their students to take an interest in how the language works and what it is like. His recommendations did not find acceptance among the public at large: facts were not to be allowed to influence opinions.

In *Facts about Current English Usage* Albert Marckwardt and Fred Walcott extended Leonard's work. They sought to further clarify the 121 usages that Leonard had classified as "disputable." They looked at the history of these usages, particularly as the *OED* had described that history, and were able to document that 106 of them were in good literary and colloquial use. Even some of Leonard's "illiterate" uses, e.g., *had awoken, he drunk, he begun, ain't, have drank,* and *you was mistaken* could be found in reputable sources. They concluded that English usage was more liberal than Leonard had said it was.

In 1940 Charles Fries published *American English Grammar,* based on thousands of handwritten letters to the United States government. He used these letters to find out exactly how Americans of different social and educational backgrounds used the language in writing rather formal letters. This study is interesting for the light it throws on exactly who uses various grammatical constructions; it is one of the best accounts we have of the grammar of written English. *American English Grammar* offers us a description of what Fries considered to be the facts of grammatical usage in the middle of twentieth-century North America and concluded that much grammar teaching had been ineffective.

In 1952 the NCTE published *The English Language Arts,* the work of a commission that it had appointed in 1945. This book tried to draw public attention to certain facts about English: language changes constantly; change is normal; the spoken language is the language; correctness rests upon usage; and all usage is relative. Such statements are behind the doctrine that has become known as "appropriateness," which says that students should be shown how to tailor their language use according to circumstance. This doctrine is itself mildly prescriptive in nature although what is

prescribed in it is variety of use. For example, the doctrine acknowledges that formal, written English has its conventions and
its uses and is entirely appropriate to these uses. What it does not
do, however, is insist that these conventions also apply to informal spoken English. This NCTE publication was severely criticized.
Who Killed Grammar? by Harry Warfel in 1952 and *The House of the
Intellect* by Jacques Barzun in 1959 strongly attacked it and linguists were blamed for the decline of grammatical study in the
schools, Barzun going so far as to name Fries as a "culprit."

If such teaching had declined it was because it had become irrelevant, as the NCTE had clearly demonstrated. However, it is
sometimes easier emotionally to attempt to kill the bearer of bad
news than to deal sensibly with that news. That is what happened: those who pointed out that much English teaching was
completely misdirected and who tried to indicate better directions
to take were assailed. Because the old way had failed, those who
said so were blamed for that failure. When *Webster's Third* was
published in 1961, another linguistic war erupted because the
battle lines had been drawn very clearly almost a decade before.

Later attempts to introduce more linguistically-oriented grammatical study into North American schools were a failure. The
new grammars relied heavily on linguistic formalisms, their terminology tended to be abstruse, they were designed for systematic rather than *ad hoc* instruction, and they emphasized
description, variation, and the spoken language. They were clearly
out of tenor with the time. Teachers who had rejected the "old
grammar" could not be persuaded that the "new grammar" had
anything better to offer their students. They may well have been
right because there is little reason to believe that the study of any
grammar, old or new, leads anyone to think better or write better. Linguists, professional students of language, are just as likely
as any other people to do silly things and write poorly.

Teaching about the language, when such teaching occurs, is
still largely within the old, outdated tradition, and the beliefs that
inform such teaching are the old ones. Many literacy programs
are confused about what they are doing because of a failure to
understand the relationship between speaking and writing. Perhaps the most difficult task of all in teaching people about lan-

guage in a culture with a tradition of literacy is getting those who do the teaching to be able to distinguish between what people say and what they write, and between statements about sounds and statements about letters, and to understand the complexity of the relationships between the two.

The origins of this difficulty are clear. Those of us who learned English as our first language have no recollection of how we learned its sounds and its grammar. We did not learn these in the way that we learned to count or to name the capitals of various countries. We did learn them or we could not have understood our parents or siblings or those teachers who set out to "teach us the language." What many of us do recollect – some quite painfully – is learning to read, spell, and write, and to use standard English. These tasks were almost certainly made more difficult than necessary for the same reason that we are still confused today. Those appointed to help us in these tasks – teachers, consultants, writers of text books, and so on – were themselves confused. The cultural lag here is enormous.

This cycle is far too often perpetuated with the blind continuing to lead the blind. The results should not surprise us. Today, much of what is taught about language in the schools is either irrelevant to the task at hand or quite false. If children do learn to read and write, that testifies more to the fact that we cannot keep them from learning something rather than to the fact that anyone thoroughly understands what is going on in language-oriented classrooms. Right from their first days in school children are asked to use concepts like "sound," "syllable," "word," and "sentence" in solving the various problems their teachers set for them. These are some of the key concepts of linguistics. Trying to figure out what sounds, syllables, words, and sentences are is a fundamental linguistic pursuit. Teachers, however, assume that they are givens and that they can rely on five- and six-year-olds' "knowing" what they are! Studies tell us that children of this age often find such concepts totally bewildering. Childen do learn to parrot certain definitions we teach them but that is an entirely different matter and the learning quite irrelevant to the task at hand.

It is not surprising that teachers behave the way they do: received wisdom exerts strong pressures. Teachers ask children to sound out *cat* by spelling it out as either *si, ay, ti* or *kuh, a, tuh* in order somehow to come up with the right pronunciation. Such a task boggles the mind but, it is, nevertheless, a task required of children every day. They instruct children to say *house* not *'ouse* or *hwen* not *wen* (for *when*) without providing any reason for doing so. They syllabify *lemon* as *lem-on* and *demon* as *de-mon* to help children arrive at the right pronunciation, but common sense tells us that if in these words we can recognize the difference between "short *e*" and "long *e* " the syllabication issue is irrelevant. So much of what is taught must seem like meaningless mumb-jumbo to those being taught.

Any teaching about the grammar of the language is likely to be laden with prescriptive injunctions. Much of it will concentrate on a few arbitrary points. Grammatical teaching does not deal with how English works. It deals with certain irregular noun, pronoun, and verb forms, some arbitrary cases of agreement, a few esoteric "rules," e.g., *I have never heard of his doing it* versus *I have never heard of him doing it*, and a variety of shibboleths. The instruction is always conducted within a pseudo-moral framework of "good" versus "bad" so that many students are led to feel that there is something essentially wrong about the way they use the language and that they cannot possibly free themselves from "linguistic original sin." What should be a liberating study of each person's most basic human characteristic often becomes the dullest, most meaningless subject in the curriculum.

When a North American tobacco company that was criticized for using *like* as a conjunction in one of its advertisements ran another which asked *What do you want, good grammar or good taste?*, we must assume it was betting that the answer would be good taste. People would not vote for good grammar. Why should they? As taught in most schools, "good grammar" must have left a bitter aftertaste that lasted for years. Perhaps this kind of "good grammar" should carry one of those warning labels: "May be harmful to your linguistic health." But since linguistic unhealth is the societal norm that is unlikely.

CHAPTER EIGHT

Future Perfect?

As we are about to enter a new millennium – although exactly when is disputed and the significance of the event is entirely a phenomenon of the world of imagination – we still have a poor understanding of language. Old beliefs linger on in our schools, colleges, and universities, and the general public is ill-informed. Furthermore, almost everyone in the media is an expert on language. If you make a living through writing and you have temporarily run out of topics to write about, write something about the English language. Journalists, writers, critics, editors, teachers of writing, and professors of this, that, or the other all feel free to write about English. Writing on almost any other topic, they would do some research, but not when writing about our language. You qualify yourself as an expert simply by speaking and writing English.

There are some "regulars" on the list. William Safire is a speech writer and political commentator who also writes essays on language for the *New York Times Sunday Magazine*. He is a self-proclaimed "language maven" – *maven* is Yiddish for "expert." Safire periodically puts his essays together in books such as *On Language* and *What's the Good Word?* He claims to be a "libertarian" in language matters and has been known to disagree with conservative rivals: for example, he accepts *hopefully* and *finalize*. Safire is one of the better informed, self-appointed experts. Edward Newman made his name in television but now passes judgment on language in books like *Strictly Speaking* and *A Civil Tongue*. Newman rejects *rather unique, hopefully,* and the use of the *-ize* suffix. He claims in the first of these books that "respect for rules has been breaking down and correct expression is considered almost a badge of dishonor." Now we are among the less well-informed.

Philip Howard writes for the London *Times* and periodically publishes his opinions on language matters in books such as *The State of the Language* and *Winged Words*. He is very sure of his opinions, telling us in the second of these books that "serious points are made and where possible the truth stated." However, much of that truth seems to be opinion in disguise. Richard Mitchell is a professor in New Jersey who calls himself the "Underground Grammarian"; he is the author of *Less than Words Can Say* and *The Leaning Tower of Babel and other Affronts by the Underground Grammarian*. Mitchell does not like *prioritize, module, facilitate, interface,* and a lot of other things too. John Simon, a critic of the arts, drama, and film, is a self-declared elitist, a person firmly convinced of the rectitude of his own judgments, and one of the harshest critics of the current state of the language. In *Paradigms Lost* Simon seems to revel in his lack of expertise in language matters.

A contempt for factual knowledge, not unsurprisingly, is widespread among most of these commentators. It takes only the smallest amount of research to show how invalid is much of what they say. To find someone like Jim Quinn, who is willing to look at facts in *American Tongue and Cheek*, is to find "the exception that proves the rule." Quinn's respect for facts leads him to conclusions that are completely at odds with those of Simon and his cohorts.

The opinions of the language mavens are very influential and are similar to those of many of our language gate-keepers. These people are conservative and prescriptivist in orientation. They see themselves as maintaining standards and as being the guardians and protectors of the language. They care about English, but they do not care about facts.

As long ago as 1921, in his inaugural lecture at Oxford, the philologist Henry Wyld pointed out that "the subject-matter of English Philology possesses a strange fascination for the man in the street, but almost everything he thinks and says about it is incredibly and hopelessly wrong. There is no subject which attracts a larger number of cranks and quacks than English Philology. In no subject, probably, is the knowledge of the educated public at a lower ebb." He added that there is a profound general ignorance in spite of the existence of a considerable mass of well-ascertained facts. Leonard Bloomfield, discussing *ain't* in his "Secondary and Tertiary Responses to Language," noted that it is not one of the fundamental problems of linguistics. "Strangely enough, people without linguistic training devote a great deal of effort to futile discussions of this topic without progressing to the study of language, which alone could give them the key." But Bloomfield seems to suggest that anything he said on the subject would be ignored anyway.

What we have are two groups of people who care about the language but care about it for different reasons and in very different ways. In the words of John Sherwood in an article entitled "Dr. Kinsey and Professor Fries" in *College English*, which discussed the "old" and "new" grammarians: "What the two grammars really reflect is two ways of looking at language, two ideals of language, and perhaps in the end two ways of life." Mario Pei expressed much the same sentiment in the *Saturday Review* in commenting on the storm that greeted the publication of *Webster's Third*: "There was far more to the controversy than met the eye, for the battle was not merely over language. It was over a whole philosophy of life."

At issue is who gets to control the language, who sets the standards. In *Paradigms Lost* Simon declares that English belongs to those "who have striven to learn it properly," which, of course, begs the question in that word *properly*. Moreover, he tells us that we should preserve *whom* if for no other reason than to show that we can force people to learn it, because without it they will remain "ignorant." Simon believes that only an elite care – or should that be *cares*? – about the language.

In Simon's view language belongs to gifted individuals like him who use it "correctly," and not to illiterates and "bodies of people forming tendentious and propagandistic interest groups, determined to use it for what they (usually mistakenly) believe to be their advantage." However, Simon himself belongs to an interest group. The English politician Enoch Powell was another with similar views. In an essay giving us some of his thoughts on grammar and syntax, he blamed a lack of knowledge of the classics and the spread of education for what he perceived to be a decline in the use of English: "The protection for the structure of English . . . is a cultural elite which has absorbed its English while being educated in Latin grammar and the Latin classics."

The language becomes a battleground for those who want to preserve what they have against those they see as wanting to take away what they have. By birth, accident, or in some cases sheer hard work, they use a particular variety of the language and they insist that others regard this variety as superior. They are determined to hold on to what power they have. They do not wish to know exactly how that variety achieved the position it did achieve. Nor can they always agree among themselves on every one of its characteristics. For them writing about language is an exercise in self-justification and self-legitimization, one in which they can set forth their own political, social, and philosophical beliefs without having to be careful about facts. They believe that they are promoting the "best" English for the best reasons. Many others accept this view and many more have it thrust upon them. It has enormous weight in our society.

People like Samuel Johnson and Noah Webster knew they had a vested interest in what they were saying and writing about the language. They deliberately advanced their own personal and class interests. They regarded themselves as pace-setters and hoped that others would follow. They succeeded beyond their wildest expectations. Their modern followers seek a similar glory.

There are good reasons to oppose the view that an uninformed elite should decide for us what is right or wrong about the language and tell us what language is. Good faith must also be attributed to another group of people who care about English, people who see the shortcomings of the uninformed, elitist position, how it perpetuates erroneous beliefs, makes rational discussion of language issues almost impossible, and confounds educational practices. This group would like to see language studied scientifically and the whole Latinate tradition with its heavy emphasis on the power of the written word reduced, possibly even abandoned.

What we have is a classic debate between the conservative and the liberal, the traditionalist and the progressivist, the authoritarian and the permissivist, and the non-scientist and the scientist. In this case the line-up on one side is consistent. The system of beliefs that controls most popular thinking about language is conservative, traditional, authoritarian, and non-scientific.

We can be sure that the debate is far from over. Small points of grammar and usage will continue to rouse people to great passion. However, great passion about small things is a recurrent feature of life. Some of us can remember the controversies in the 1960s about miniskirts, and long hair on males. What passions they brought forth! One of America's leading social-advice columnists once pointed out that the particular issue that generated some of her largest correspondence concerned whether you should hang a roll of toilet paper with the loose sheets on the outside or on the inside. This concern with trivia should remind us of Jonathan Swift's Big-endians and Little-endians and, of course, all that Swift intended to satirize thereby, all those trivial religious, social, and political issues for which countless millions have perished over the centuries.

We do not, after all, live in a rational world. It is, as Carl Sagan reminds us, "demon-haunted" for great numbers of people. It is a world in which a 1994 Gallup survey found that over 70 percent of American adults believed in miracles, hell, and angels, and over 60 percent in the existence of the Devil. In *Verbal Hygiene* Deborah Cameron says that much of our behavior toward language derives from the irrationality of life as we experience it. So it is not surprising that we do not trust language and want to tinker with it.

Small linguistic points become symbolic of larger issues. The points are not important in themselves. It is what they can be made to symbolize that is important. Only in this way does it make sense to see any significance at all in whether we should say *Lay down, Fido* or *Lie down, Fido*. Fido is certainly quite indifferent. We may not be indifferent about the choice of words here but we should not deceive ourselves into believing that an important linguistic issue is at stake. There is an issue to be sure but it is entirely a social one.

---

1 *Mea Culpa*

Linguists cannot continue to ignore the fact that the study of language has been so utterly trivialized in the popular mind and be satisfied with having constructed their own safe retreat, a discipline in which they talk only to each other. Language is too important to be left to non-linguists to have their way with. It is too important to be left to the prescriptivists who seek to use language to put others in their place. Linguists must involve themselves in debates about the need to adopt a scientific attitude to language issues that can and should be investigated scientifically. Many educated people know more about space and time, uncertainty, and quantum effects than they do about nouns and verbs.

We live in a world in which language has been allowed to divide us, one in which death and destruction can be visited on others simply because they speak another language. Yet we worry about using *like* as a conjunction! There are issues here that all of us must address.

Caliban did not find learning language a liberating experience. Now we may understand why: we find ourselves trapped in all that goes along with that learning. A comprehensive study of language must not only describe what language is but also what we allow it to do to us. Language is far too important for us to leave alone, or to the mavens, or even to linguists. Perhaps the next millennium will bring some changes and we will achieve a more rational understanding of language in all its manifestations. That is what new years, new centuries, and new millennia are for: starting anew. We might be wise to begin the new era by taking a fresh look at how so many of us view our language.

Bibliography

Modern cited sources

Aitchison, J. *The Language Web*. Cambridge: Cambridge University Press, 1997.

Barzun, J. *The House of the Intellect*. New York: Harper & Row, 1959.

Bickerton, D. *Language and Species*. Chicago: University of Chicago Press, 1990.

Blackburn, B. *Words Fail Us*. Toronto: McClelland & Stewart, 1993.

Blamires, H. *Correcting Your English*. London: Bloomsbury, 1996.

Bloomfield, L. Why a Linguistic Society? *Language*, 1: 1–5, 1925.

——. Literate and Illiterate Speech. *American Speech*, 2: 432–8, 1927.

——. *Language*. New York: Holt, 1933.

——. Secondary and Tertiary Responses to Language. *Language*, 20: 45–55, 1944.

Bolinger, D. L. *Language, the Loaded Weapon: The Use and Abuse of Language Today*. New York: Longman, 1980.

Broadfoot, B. *Six War Years, 1939–1945*. Toronto: Doubleday, 1974.

Burchfield, R. *The Spoken Word: A BBC Guide*. London: Oxford University Press, 1982.

Cameron, D. *Verbal Hygiene*. London: Routledge, 1995.

Cheever, B., ed. *The Letters of John Cheever*. New York: Simon and Schuster, 1988.

Chomsky, N. *Cartesian Linguistics: A Chapter in the History of Rationalist Thought*. New York: Harper & Row, 1966.

Cipolla, C. M. *Literacy and Development in the West*. Harmondsworth: Penguin, 1969.

Crystal, D. *Who Cares about English Usage?* Harmondsworth: Penguin, 1984.

Dauzat, A. *Le Génie de la langue française*. Paris: Payot, 1944.

Delbanco, N. *Running in Place: Scenes from the South of France*. New York:

Atlantic Monthly Press, 1989.

Eco, U. *The Search for the Perfect Language*. Oxford: Basil Blackwell, 1995.

Evans, B. But What's a Dictionary For? *Atlantic Monthly*, 57–62, May 1962.

Fee, M. and J. McAlpine, eds. *Guide to Canadian English Usage*. Toronto: Oxford University Press, 1997.

Follett, W. Sabotage in Springfield. *Atlantic Monthly*, 73–7, January 1962.

Fowler, H. W. *A Dictionary of Modern English Usage*. Oxford: Clarendon Press, 1926.

Fries, C. C. *American English Grammar*. New York: Appleton-Century-Crofts, 1940.

Gelb, I. J. *A Study of Writing*. 2nd edn. Chicago: University of Chicago Press, 1963.

Gell-Mann, M. *The Quark and the Jaguar: Adventures in the Simple and the Complex*. New York: W. H. Freeman, 1994.

Gilman, E. W., ed. *Webster's Dictionary of English Usage*. Springfield, Mass.: Merriam-Webster, 1989.

Goody, J. R., ed. *Literacy in Traditional Societies*. Cambridge: Cambridge University Press, 1968.

Gould, S. J. *Questioning the Millennium: A Rationalist's Guide to a Precisely Arbitrary Countdown*. New York: Harmony, 1997.

Grove, V. *The Language Bar*. London: Routledge & Kegan Paul, 1950.

Hall, R. A., Jr. *Linguistics and Your Language*. Garden City, NY: Anchor, 1960.

Harris, R. S. *English Studies at Toronto: A History*. Toronto: University of Toronto Press, 1988.

Havelock, E. *The Literate Revolution in Greece and Its Cultural Consequences*. Princeton: Princeton University Press, 1982.

Hawking, S. *A Brief History of Time: From the Big Bang to Black Holes*. New York: Bantam, 1988.

Hoggart, R. *The Uses of Literacy: Aspects of Working-Class Life with Special Reference to Publications and Entertainments*. New York: Oxford University Press, 1970.

Honey, J. *Does Accent Matter?: The Pygmalion Factor*. London: Faber & Faber, 1989.

——. *Language is Power: The Story of Standard English and its Enemies*. London: Faber & Faber, 1997.

Howard, P. *The State of the Language: English Observed*. New York: Oxford University Press, 1985.

——. *Winged Words*. London: Hamish Hamilton, 1988.

Jagemann, H. C. von. Philology and Purism, *PMLA*, 15: 74–96, 1900.

Jespersen, O. *Mankind, Nation, and Individual from a Linguistic Point of View.* Cambridge, Mass.: Harvard University Press, 1925.

——. *Growth and Structure of the English Language.* 9th edn. Oxford: Basil Blackwell, 1952.

Jones, D. *English Pronouncing Dictionary.* London: Dent, 1919.

Law, V. Language and Its Students: The History of Linguistics. In N. E. Collinge, ed. *An Encyclopaedia of Language.* London: Routledge, 1990.

Leonard, S. A. *The Doctrine of Correctness in English Usage 1700–1800.* Madison: University of Wisconsin Studies in Language and Literature, No. 25, 1929.

——. *Current English Usage.* Chicago: Inland, 1932.

Logan, R. K. *The Alphabet Effect: The Impact of the Phonetic Alphabet on the Development of Western Civilization.* New York: William Morrow, 1986.

Marckwardt, A. and F. Walcott. *Facts about Current English Usage.* New York: Appleton-Century-Crofts, 1938.

Marenbon, J. *English Our English: The New Orthodoxy Examined.* London: Centre for Policy Studies, 1987.

McLuhan, M. *The Gutenberg Galaxy: The Making of Typographic Man.* Toronto: University of Toronto Press, 1962.

Meech, S. B. Early Applications of Latin Grammar to English. *PMLA*, 50: 1012–32, 1935.

Mencken, H. L. *The American Language.* New York: Knopf, 1919.

Michael, I. *English Grammatical Categories and the Tradition to 1800.* Cambridge: Cambridge University Press, 1970.

Mitchell, R. *Less than Words Can Say.* Boston: Little, Brown, 1979.

——. *The Leaning Tower of Babel and other Affronts by the Underground Grammarian.* Boston: Little, Brown, 1984.

Mittins, W. H., M. Salu, M. Edmonson, and S. Coyne. *Attitudes to English Usage.* London: Oxford University Press, 1970.

Mornet, D. *Histoire de la clarté française.* Paris: Payot, 1929.

Morris, W. and M. Morris. *Harper Dictionary of Contemporary Usage.* New York: Harper & Row, 1975.

National Council of Teachers of English. *The English Language Arts.* New York: Appleton-Century-Crofts, 1952.

Newman, E. *Strictly Speaking: Will America be the Death of English?* Indianapolis: Bobbs-Merrill, 1974.

——. *A Civic Tongue.* Indianapolis: Bobbs-Merrill, 1976.

Newmayer, F. J. *Linguistic Theory in America.* 2nd edn. New York: Academic Press, 1987.

Nunberg, G. What the Usage Panel Thinks. In C. Ricks and L. Michaels, eds. *The State of the Language.* Berkeley: University of California Press, 1990.

Orwell, G. *The Collected Essays, Journalism, and Letters of George Orwell. Vol. 4.* New York: Harcourt Brace Jovanovich, 1968.

Pattison, R. *On Literacy: The Politics of the Word from Homer to the Age of Rock.* New York: Oxford University Press, 1982.

Pedersen, H. *The Discovery of Language: Linguistic Science in the Nineteenth Century.* Reprinted. Bloomington: Indiana University Press, 1962.

Pei, M. A Loss for Words, *Saturday Review*, 82–4, November 14, 1964.

——. *Invitation to Linguistics: A Basic Introduction to the Science of Language.* Garden City, NY: Doubleday, 1965.

Piercy, M. *Summer People.* London: Michael Joseph, 1989.

Pinker, S. *The Language Instinct: How the Mind Creates Language.* New York: William Morrow, 1994.

Powell J. E. Further Thoughts: Grammar and Syntax. In C. Ricks and L. Michaels, eds. *The State of the Language.* Berkeley: University of California Press, 1990.

Quinn, J. *American Tongue and Cheek A Populist Guide to our Language.* New York: Pantheon, 1980.

Quirk, R. *The Use of English.* 2nd edn. London: Longman, 1968.

——, S. Greenbaum, G. Leech, and J. Svartvik. *A Comprehensive Grammar of the English Language.* London: Longman, 1985.

Reader's Digest. *The Right Word at the Right Time.* London: Reader's Digest Association, 1985.

Roberts, P. *The Classic Slum: Salford Life in the First Quarter of the Century.* Manchester: Manchester University Press, 1971.

Safire, W. *On Language.* New York: Times Books, 1980.

——. *What's the Good Word?* New York: Times Books, 1982.

——. *Coming to Terms.* New Your: Henry Holt, 1991.

Sagan, C. *The Demon-Haunted World: Science as a Candle in the Dark.* New York: Random House, 1996.

Sapir, E. *Language: An Introduction to the Study of Speech.* New York: Harcourt, 1921.

Saussure, F. de. *Course in General Linguistics.* London: Fontana, 1974.

Sherwood, J. C. Dr. Kinsey and Professor Fries. *College English*, 21: 275–80, 1960.

Simon, J. *Paradigms Lost.* New York: Clarkson Potter, 1980.

Steiner, G. *After Babel: Aspects of Language and Translation.* New York: Oxford University Press, 1975.

Strunk, W., Jr, and E. B. White. *The Elements of Style.* 2nd edn. New York: Macmillan, 1972.

Tibbetts, A., and C. Tibbetts. *What's Happening to American English?* New York: Charles Scribner, 1978.

Tucker, S. I. *Protean Shape: A Study in Eighteenth-Century Vocabulary and Usage.* London: The Athlone Press, 1967.

Turner, M. *Reading Minds: The Study of English in the Age of Cognitive Science.* Princeton: Princeton University Press, 1991.

Vossler, K. *The Spirit of Language in Civilization.* London. Kegan Paul, Trench, Trubner & Co., 1932.

Warfel, H. R. *Who Killed Grammar?* Gainesville: University of Florida Press, 1952.

Wilson, A. N. *Gentlemen in England.* London: Hamish Hamilton, 1985.

Wyld, H. C. *English Philology in English Universities.* Oxford: Clarendon Press, 1921.

——. *The Best English: A Claim for the Superiority of Received Standard English.* Oxford: Clarendon Press, 1934.

Selected uncited sources

Aarsleff, H. *The Study of Language in England, 1780-1860.* Princeton: Princeton University Press, 1967.

——. From Locke to Saussure: *Essays on the Study of Language and Intellectual History.* Minneapolis: University of Minnesota Press, 1982.

Abelson, P. *The Seven Liberal Arts: A Study in Mediaeval Culture.* New York: Teachers College, 1906.

Alston, R. C. *A Bibliography of the English Language from the Invention of Printing to the Year 1800.* Leeds: E. J. Arnold, 1965.

Altick, R. D. *The English Common Reader: A Social History of the Mass Reading Public, 1800–1900.* Chicago: University of Chicago Press, 1957.

Andressen J. T. *Linguistics in America 1769-1924: A Critical History.* London: Routledge, 1990.

Applebee, A. N. *Tradition and Reform in the Teaching of English: A History.* Urbana: National Council of Teachers of English, 1974.

Aston, M. Lollardy and Literacy. *History,* 62: 347–71, 1967.

Auerbach, E. *Literary Language and Its Public in Late Latin Antiquity and in the Middle Ages.* London: Routledge & Kegan Paul, 1965.

Bailey, R. W. *Images of English: A Cultural History of the Language.* Ann Arbor: University of Michigan Press, 1991.

Baron, D. E. *Grammar and Good Taste: Reforming the American Language.* New Haven: Yale University Press, 1982.

Bejoint, H. *Tradition and Innovation in Modern Dictionaries.* Oxford: Oxford University Press, 1994.

Berlin, J. A. *Rhetoric and Reality: Writing Instruction in American Colleges, 1900-1985.* Carbondale: Southern Illinois University Press, 1987.

Blake, N. F. *Non-Standard Language in English Literature*. London: André Deutsch, 1981.

Bolton, W. F., ed. *The English Language: Essays by English and American Men of Letters 1490–1839*. Cambridge: Cambridge University Press, 1966.

Burchfield, R. *Unlocking the English Language*. New York: Hill and Wang, 1991.

Burke, P. *Popular Culture in Early Modern Europe*. New York: Harper & Row, 1978.

Calvet, L.-J. *La Guerre des langues et les politiques linguistiques*. Paris: Payot, 1987.

Castell, S. de, A. Luke, and K. Egan, eds. *Literacy, Society, and Schooling: A Reader*. Cambridge: Cambridge University Press, 1986.

Charlton, K. *Education in Renaissance England*. London: Routledge & Kegan Paul, 1965.

Clanchy, M. *From Memory to Written Record: England 1066–1307*. London: Arnold, 1979.

Clarke, M. L. *Classical Education in Britain 1500–1900*. Cambridge: Cambridge University Press, 1959.

Cmiel, K. *Democratic Eloquence: The Fight over Popular Speech in Nineteenth-Century America*. New York: William Morrow, 1990.

Cobban, A. B. *The Medieval English Universities: Oxford and Cambridge to c.1500*. Aldershot: Scolar Press, 1988.

Cohen, M. *Sensible Words: Linguistic Practice in England 1640–1785*. Baltimore: Johns Hopkins University Press, 1977.

Cooper, R. L. *Language Planning and Social Change*. Cambridge: Cambridge University Press, 1989.

Court. F. E. *Institutionalizing English Literature: The Culture and Politics of Literary Study, 1750–1900*. Stanford: Stanford University Press, 1992.

Cressy, D. L. *Literacy and the Social Order: Reading and Writing in Tudor and Stuart England*. Cambridge: Cambridge University Press, 1980.

Crowley, T. *The Politics of Discourse: The Standard Language Question in British Cultural Debates*. London: Macmillan, 1989.

———. *Proper English? Readings in Language, History and Cultural Identity*. London: Routledge, 1991.

Crystal, D. *The Cambridge Encyclopedia of the English Language*. Cambridge: Cambridge University Press, 1995.

Daniels, H. A. *Famous Last Words: The American Language Crisis Reconsidered*. Carbondale: Southern Illinois University Press, 1983.

Davies, W. J. F. *Teaching Reading in Early England*. London: Pitman, 1973.

Demers, P. *Heaven upon Earth: The Form of Moral and Religious Children's*

Literature, to 1850. Knoxville: University of Tennessee Press, 1993.

DeMolen, R. L. *Richard Mulcaster (c.1531–1611) and Educational Reform in the Renaissance.* Niewkoop: De Graaf, 1991.

Dixon, J. A. *Schooling in 'English': Critical Episodes in the Struggle to Shape Literary and Cultural Studies.* Milton Keynes: Open University Press, 1991.

Dowling, L. Victorian Oxford and the Science of Language. *PMLA*, 97:2:160–78, 1982.

Drake, G. *The Role of Prescriptivism in American Linguistics, 1820–1970.* Amsterdam: John Benjamins,1979.

Dubois, C-G. *Mythe et langage au seizième siècle.* Bordeaux; Ducrois, 1970.

Dykema, K. W. Where Our Grammar Came From. *College English,* 22: 455–65, 1961.

Eisenstein, E. L. *The Printing Revolution in Early Modern Europe.* Cambridge: Cambridge University Press, 1983.

Elsky, M. *Authorizing Words: Speech, Writing, and Print in the English Renaissance.* Ithaca: Cornell University Press, 1989.

Febvre, L. and H-J. Martin. *The Coming of the Book: The Impact of Printing 1450-1800.* London: NLB, 1976.

Finegan, E. *Attitudes Toward English Usage: The History of a War of Words.* New York: Teachers College Press, 1980.

Fisher, J. L. Chancery and the Emergence of Standard Written English in the Fifteenth Century. *Speculum,* 52: 870–99, 1977.

Fries, C. C. Rules of the Common School Grammars. *PMLA,* 42, 221–37, 1927.

Graff, G. *Professing Literature: An Institutional History.* Chicago: University of Chicago Press, 1987.

Graff, H., ed. *Literacy and Social Development in the West: A Reader.* Cambridge: Cambridge University Press, 1981.

——. *The Legacies of Literacy: Continuities and Contradictions in Western Culture and Society.* Bloomington: Indiana University Press, 1987.

Green, J. *Chasing the Sun: Dictionary-makers and the Dictionaries They Made.* London: Pimlico, 1997.

Greenbaum, S., ed. *The English Language Today.* Oxford: Pergamon Press, 1985.

Guitarte, G. L. and Q. R. Torres. Linguistic Correctness and the Role of the Academies. *Current Trends in Linguistics,* 4: 562–604, 1967.

Haas, W. *Standard Languages: Spoken and Written.* Manchester: Manchester University Press, 1982.

Harris, R. A. *The Linguistics Wars.* New York: Oxford University Press, 1993.

Bibliography

Hartung, C. V. The Persistence of Tradition in Grammar. *Quarterly Journal of Speech*, 48: 176–86, 1962.

Hayashi, T. *The Theory of English Lexicography 1530–1791*. Amsterdam: John Benjamins, 1978.

Heath, S. B. A National Language Academy? Debate in the New Nation. *Linguistics*, 189: 9–43, 1977.

Jackson, M. V. *Engines of Instruction, Mischief, and Magic: Children's Literature in England from Its Beginnings to 1835*. Lincoln: University of Nebraska Press, 1989.

Jones, R. F. *The Triumph of the English Language*. Stanford: Stanford University Press, 1953.

Joseph, J. E. *Eloquence and Power: The Rise of Language Standards and Standard Languages*. London: Frances Pinter, 1987.

—— and T. J. Taylor, eds. *Ideologies of Language*. London: Routledge, 1990.

Juliard, P. *Philosophies of Language in Eighteenth-Century France*. The Hague: Mouton, 1970.

Kitzhaber, A. R. *Rhetoric in American Colleges, 1850–1900*. Dallas: Southern Methodist University Presss, 1990.

Knight, I F. *The Geometric Spirit: The Abbé Condillac and the French Enlightenment*. New Haven: Yale University Press, 1968.

Leith, D. *A Social History of English*, 2nd edn. London: Routledge, 1997.

Lockridge, K. A. *Literacy in Colonial New England*. New York: Norton, 1974.

Lowenthal, L. *Literature, Popular Culture and Society*. Englewood Cliffs, NJ: Prentice-Hall, 1961.

Lyman R. L. *English Grammar in American Schools Before 1850*. United States Department of Interior, Bureau of Education, Bulletin, 1921, No. 12, 1922.

Martin, H.-J. *The History and Power of Writing*. Chicago: University of Chicago Press, 1994.

Mathieson, M. *The Preachers of Culture: A Study of English and Its Teachers*. London: George Allen & Unwin, 1975.

McArthur, T. ed. *The Oxford Companion to the English Language*. Oxford: Oxford University Press, 1992.

McMurtry, J. *English Language, English Literature: The Creation of an Academic Discipline*. Hamden, Conn.: Archon Books, 1985.

Michael, I. *The Teaching of English: From the Sixteenth Century to 1870*. Cambridge: Cambridge University Press, 1987.

Milroy, J. and L. Milroy. *Authority in Language*. London: Routledge & Kegan Paul, 1985.

Morton, H. C. *The Story of Webster's Third: Philip Gove's Controversial Dictionary and Its Critics*. Cambridge: Cambridge University Press, 1994.

Neuberg, V. E. *The Penny Histories: A Study of Chapbooks for Young Readers over Two Centuries.* London: Oxford University Press, 1968.

——. *Popular Education in Eighteenth Century England.* London: Woburn Press, 1971.

Newbolt, H. *The Teaching of English in England.* London: HMSO, 1921.

Ohmann, R. *English in America: A Radical View of the Profession.* New York: Oxford University Press, 1976.

Ong, W. J. *Orality and Literacy: The Technologizing of the Word.* London: Methuen, 1982.

Orme, N. *Education and Society in Medieval and Renaissance England.* London: Hambledon Press, 1989.

Padley, G. A. *Grammatical Theory in Western Europe, 1500–1700: The Latin Tradition.* Cambridge: Cambridge University Press, 1976.

Paetow, L. J. *The Arts Course at Medieval Universities with Special Reference to Grammar and Rhetoric.* Champaign: University of Illinois, 1910.

Palmer, D. J. *The Rise of English Studies: An Account of the Study of English Language and Literature from Its Origins to the Making of the Oxford English School.* London: Oxford University Press, 1965.

Reddick, A. *The Making of Johnson's Dictionary.* Cambridge: Cambridge University Press, 1990.

Riche, P. *Education and Culture in the Barbarian West.* Columbia: University of South Carolina Press, 1976.

Rickard, P. *The Embarrassments of Irregularity: The French Language in the Eighteenth Century.* Cambridge: Cambridge University Press, 1982.

Robins, R. H. *A Short History of Linguistics.* 3rd edn. London: Longman, 1990.

Rollins, R. M. *The Long Journey of Noah Webster.* Philadelphia: University of Pennsylvania Press, 1980.

Scaglione, A., ed. *The Emergence of National Languages.* Ravenna: Longo, 1984.

Scragg, D. G. *A History of English Spelling.* Manchester: Manchester University Press, 1975.

Shayer, D. *The Teaching of English in Schools 1900–1970.* London: Routledge & Kegan Paul, 1972.

Simpson, D. *The Politics of American English, 1776–1850.* New York: Oxford University Press, 1986.

Sledd, J. H. and G. J. Colb. *Dr Johnson's Dictionary.* Chicago: University of Chicago Press, 1955.

—— and W. R. Ebbitt, eds. *Dictionaries and THAT Dictionary.* Chicago: Scott, Foresman, 1962.

Smith, O. *The Politics of Language 1791–1819.* Oxford: Clarendon Press, 1984.

Soltow, L. and E. Stevens. *The Rise of Literacy and the Common School in the United States: A Socioeconomic Analysis to 1870*. Chicago: University of Chicago Press, 1981.

Spufford, M. *Small Books and Pleasant Histories: Popular Fiction and Its Readership in Seventeenth-Century England*. London: Methuen, 1981.

Stock, B. *The Implications of Literacy*. Princeton: Princeton University Press, 1983.

Stone. L. Literacy and Education in England 1640-1900. *Past and Present*, 42: 69–139, 1969.

Tucker, S. I. *English Examined: Two Centuries of Comment on the Mother-Tongue*. Cambridge: Cambridge University Press, 1961.

Vincent, D. *Literacy and Popular Culture: England 1750–1914*. Cambridge: Cambridge University Press, 1989.

Warfel, H. R. *Noah Webster: Schoolmaster to America*. New York: Macmillan, 1936.

Watson, F. *The English Grammar Schools to 1600: Their Curiculum and Practice*. Cambridge: Cambridge University Press. 1908.

Webb, R. K. *The British Working Class Reader 1790–1848*. London: George Allen & Unwin, 1955.

Index